Eighth Circle of Hell

www.dianahiebauthor.com

Eighth Circle of Hell

A Woman

v

The English Family Court

Diana Hieb

This book achieved completion with faith and perseverance on an old and continuously overheating laptop with a faulty keyboard.

It is now in your hands for the grace of the heavenly power which loves us all.

Copyright © 2023 Diana Hieb.
All Rights Reserved.

Diana Hieb has asserted her right under the Copyright, Designs and Patents Act 1988 to be identified as the author of this work.

A CIP catalogue record for this book is available from the British Library.

All rights reserved, including the right to reproduce this book, or portions thereof in any form. No part of this text may be reproduced, transmitted, downloaded, decompiled, reverse engineered, or stored, in any form or introduced into any information storage and retrieval system, in any form or by any means, whether electronic or mechanical without the express written permission of the author or publisher.

Paperback ISBN: 978-1-3999-5189-0
An eBook version is also available on Amazon Kindle.

Cover Image: 'Journey' by Sharif Amer.
Typeset in Adobe Garamond Pro.
Printed and bound by Clays Ltd, Elcograf S.p.A.

"The ultimate tragedy is not the oppression and cruelty by the bad people, but the silence over that by the good people."

MARTIN LUTHER KING JR.

CONTENTS

Dedication xi

Acknowledgements xiii

About the Author xv

Preface xix

Chapter 1: Women Like Us 3

Chapter 2: Early Life 15

Chapter 3: My Family 27

Chapter 4: The House 33

Chapter 5: Bittersweet 43

    Mercedes' Birthday 46

    Texas 50

Chapter 6: Should I Stay? 59

    A Will? 82

    The Divine Power Has My Back 90

Chapter 7: The Abuser 97

    Deception 99

    Stein and His Companies 103

    Bewildered and Sad 113

    Dr. Zaidi 121

Chapter 8: Goodbye Michael 131

Chapter 9: The Legal Firms 143

- Camilla Fusco and Anthony Gold Solicitors 143
- Stewarts Law 152
- Vardags 164

Chapter 10: Fraud, Perjury and Mockery 171
- The Big Lie 176

Chapter 11: In the Land of Nothingness 199
- Irony 209
- Action Fraud 213
- Displaced 214

Chapter 12: Discrimination 229
- Worth Reading 229
- Eyes Windows of the Soul 238
- Cutting My Wins or Rising Phoenix? 240
- The Wrong Judge 242
- The Regulators 247
- Important Things in Life 250
- The Legal of the Illegal 253

Chapter 13: Reflections 265

Notes 273

Dedication

This book is dedicated to those who did not get to see justice from the family court. Who gave up for the sake of keeping their sanity. Who felt alone, abandoned, discriminated against and ignored. To my beautiful and caring mother; you are special beyond believe. For my children Steven, David and Diana-Mercedes, who blossomed into beautiful, caring souls, despite enduring years of their father's narcissistic abuse. For my older brother Francisco and my nephew, who passed away. During my divorce litigation, they, too, suffered the abuse of my ex-husband. I miss them very much, and they will never be forgotten. And for all those who are currently facing the injustice of the family court, I say to you, do not give up. You are not alone. Don't give up, because bigger changes and achievements come around when we persist.

Acknowledgements

I will forever be grateful to Asunción Doral Coaching, Maggie Tumembatur, Sandy and Jia Lu, Yunany Adams and Javier Rosales, Leonora Stavrianakos, Ms. Madupe, Mr. Luqman Thomas, Debra Russell, Aralis Rodríguez, Sharif Ahmed for crating the piece of art for my book cover; may the world learn about your art and how strong you are despite adversity. To Dr. Amanda and Principal GP Dr. McDaid for never failing to care for me and following up with my progress in overcoming depression and health issues. To Solace Women's Aid and all their kind volunteers, Nikos and Shoreh Kaloyeropoulos, Claus and Lorena Schieber, Nilda Gonzales de Leon, and George Mukas. To Dr. Steven Greer for allowing me to step into consciousness and for dedicating your life to disclosure and a better world. To Medical Medium for reinforcing my ancestors' teachings that most of the answers to curing illness are found in nature. To Gaia for the fantastic set of experts in their field ready to share their knowledge and help humanity unlock its utmost potential and reclaim its rightful place in the universe, and YOU for taking the time to read my story.

About the Author

Diana finished her primary school years in Guatemala. Due to the civil war and to continue her college and university studies, her family sent her to New York, where she achieved a degree in microcomputers and business administration. Diana completed an internship at Pfizer headquarters in Manhattan, New York, and soon after received a job offer with the pharmaceutical giant. Pursuing her love for creativity and the arts whilst working full-time and caring for two young children, she pursued a degree in graphic design with a minor in photography. Diana also founded a photography business in New York City during her entrepreneurial life. She landed jobs in companies such as FactSet, a significant financial research company that offers risk analytics tools and real-time data feeds for institutional investors. The United Nations cultural event unit invited her to exhibit her project "Eyes Windows of the Soul".

Grabbing her bags and relocating whenever required by her ex-husband did not prevent Diana from continuing her commitment to helping others and growing her curious mind. As soon as landing in London, she became part of the Kensington and Chelsea Women's clubs and enrolled to support charities such as Centre Point, which aids young people running away from abuse and escaping homelessness. She also helped a school for adults seeking to learn essential reading and writing skills in Antigua, Guatemala.

In 2014, Diana once again had to relocate, this time to Hong Kong. Soon after, becoming the President of the Asociación the Mujeres de Habla Hispana AMHH or Association of Spanish Speaking Women in Hong Kong and an ambassador between consulates and embassies, creating and promoting cultural events and aiding many Spanish-speaking community members during their ex-pat permanence in Hong Kong. She was essential in organizing aid for Cradle of Hope, an orphanage in Macao founded and managed by a Brazilian couple. Pursuing her motto of a win-win situation, she founded a company in Hong Kong to help promote organic coffee, macadamia, and cocoa bean from small to medium size growers in her motherland. Besides overseeing her company's growth, after her role as President of AMHH, she continued to support and visit prisoners in Hong Kong who spoke Spanish, English, and Portuguese. Diana sourced and distributed reading material and promoted drawing as an empowering medium of expression and alleviating isolation and stress. She supported drawing competitions among inmates. During the pandemic, Diana enlisted with the National Health Insurance (NHS) in England as a Volunteer First Respondent and remained faithful to her commitment for two years until the program ended.

"If no one remembers you for at least one good thing you have done after you are gone, you have not been here".

Preface

When you are a victim of a narcissistic individual, you face horrifying mental and physical abuse which society frequently doesn't see. If you find yourself in the Family Court framework with that individual, you subsequently deal with unlimited stress and terror, which people do not take notice of. To be caught in a pattern of abuse and to be hurt and silenced by a brutal and unreasonable system makes you endure enormous pain.

If you think about every single occasion in your life where you have confronted trauma and remind yourself that the storm always passes in the end, you will rise out of the darkness and into the light. In time, you will smile again. You acquired strength of mind, clarity, and insight from the darkness and developed as an individual as you withstood the hardship. Time and persistence mend many injuries that grow you out of your trauma, and good things happen when you least expect it. Hold it together, my friend. You will evolve out of this as well.

PREFACE

Violence against women and young girls is one of the world's most common human rights violations, occurring every day worldwide. It has short and long-term physical, financial, and mental effects on people, preventing their full and equivalent participation in society. The extent of its effect, both on the lives of people and communities overall, is endless. This book is for women like Valerie Bacot, who faced 20 years of abuse and were ignored by the police and society. Like her, I have also been victimized, only because I was honest, relentless, and stood in the face of injustice to say, "No more."

The development of emotional distress, impotence and distrust toward the mere entity that was supposed to protect me and my rights has been a traumatic chapter of my life. I hope that the personal account of my experience will help to expose the truth of my ordeal to those who can relate to me.

"Our lives begin to end the day we become silent about things that matter."

MARTIN LUTHER KING JR.

Eighth Circle of Hell

Chapter 1

Women Like Us

The most critical exercises in life come from stories, regardless of whether these be nursery rhymes or children's tales read to us by our parents, illustrations from holy books, moral stories or inspirational books.

Since I was a child, I had a fantasy about changing the world, yet growing up, I had no clue how to manage my own life, let alone change the world.

That is exactly when I started to realize that all the change I was looking for in my life had to initially begin with me. In order to bring about any change within me, I had to associate with my internal identity and develop self-esteem. Therefore, the key is to begin a relationship with yourself first and foremost. Becoming settled in your own skin is simply the most valuable gift you can give yourself. There are two angles here: arriving at this state and maintaining it. The truth is that any day is less complicated than the next. It supports that condition of harmony regardless of hardships from the external world, and that is a test. Change within, and the external circumstances improve.

The sooner you gain proficiency with this the better, and the sooner you acknowledge this fact, the sooner you will need to figure out how you can change. In this regard, Rumi's expressive words ring so true:

> "Yesterday, you were clever, so you wanted to change the world. Today you are wise, so you're changing yourself."[1]

Some of the things I want to write about in this book are the hardships of life. Believe it or not, life is like this—the reality of life, I mean. The entire social justice system is unfair. Our comprehension of social justice is inseparably associated with our meaning of terms like equality and opportunity and clearing policy questions regarding the general responsibilities and commitments of people and society. Originally, the possibility of social justice was group-specific—that is, it was applied exclusively to a specific group or country determined to review the impacts of hierarchal inequalities, especially inherited inequalities.

I don't want this book to be a cause of depression to anybody; rather, my purpose is to spread awareness and share the beauty of watching myself grow up. I want people to know the beauty of my childhood. Before getting

CHAPTER 1: WOMEN LIKE US

into every hardship and struggle I have experienced, I would like this colorful time to remain in your mind.

So, let's begin by telling you who I am. I grew up in Guatemala, which is a Central American country south of Mexico and next to Belize, which holds the second-largest barrier reef in the world. Belize was first part of Guatemala, and later, it became a British colony. From the mid-nineteenth century, it was called British Honduras by the English invaders until 1973, when the British colonial office officially named it Belize.

It was then "decided" that it would become independent after a dispute between Guatemala and Great Britain. Guatemala has gorgeous views of the Caribbean and Pacific Ocean.

I grew up in the countryside next to three majestic volcanoes. My family have been living there for 200 years. We grew up close to great grandpa Diego. He was an interesting character in the family, always positive and hopeful. When he reached the age of 100, I asked Grandpa Diego how it felt to be so old, to which he replied,

"Age is a figurative thought in your head; the day you decide to grow up, you are officially old."

He had almost everything in his pockets: plasters/band-aids, Vicks ointment, aspirin, chewing gum, and candies that made us jump up and down with joy when he gave them to us. My siblings and I used to joke that his pockets were bottomless or at least ankle-length. Grandpa Diego used to tell us stories about a time long ago. He loved hot chilis, smoked a cigar and had black coffee at 3 p.m. every day. The weather in Guatemala is implausible, the reason why it's called the "Land of Eternal Spring", crisp sunny mornings, warm afternoons and cool nights for a perfect sleep.

About my parents, my father is a retired mechanical engineer who was hired as quality labor and worked for local government in New York since 1968. My Mom went through a lot. When she was only 16, she got into an arranged marriage with a wealthy man ten years her senior, only to become a widow five years into the marriage. Four years later, when Mom and Dad met, it was love at first sight. My little brother and I are children from Mom's second marriage.

As a girl, I used to be happy, independent, and very different from my siblings—the rebel in the house. I was literally a tomboy growing up. I had a five year younger brother, four years older brother and two older sisters. There was a big age gap between my sisters and me, so we never really clicked. But overall, we all lived happily together. When I think of my childhood, I remember having messy, soft curls, wearing pale-yellow dress and psychedelic-color tights. But my favorite fashion statement was a pair of patent yellow leather ankle-high boots, a fashionista, no doubt.

In the 70s, I remember running around with boys and racing with dogs, reading poetry, loving classical music and being a perfectionist at the same time. My Mom would often tease me that I did not belong to our family. My four siblings were so well-behaved,

CHAPTER 1: WOMEN LIKE US

but little Diana was always in trouble. I loved to be out of the house playing in our block with boys, running with our dogs and climbing trees. My Mom often threatened me.

"I'm going to tie you to a tree if I wake up after siesta and find you on the street playing."

She was always worried about me not growing up lady-like.

One day she caught me. I had finished my homework extremely fast and gone to play outside. She found me in the street, dragged me home and tied me to a tree in the garden. I cried for a while and threatened to run away. I mean, I was seven years old. After a short while, my mom untied me. While she was preparing dinner, my neighborhood friends began whistling outside my door, and I went out again! We played marbles and hide and seek. Despite the punishment, I became the old me, forgetting that my mom had asked me not to go out. And that is when my mom realized I was a lost case. Mom once told me that she could predict I would be an excellent door-to-door salesperson because I loved roaming the streets.

In the Mayan and Kaqchikel native cultures in Guatemala, it is said that every child is born with specific virtues to help their path in this world. We must not alter, void, or undermine them as they are the "tools" needed for their journey. I am grateful for the personality I received and for my parents for letting me keep and develop my tools for my very own path.

Getting back to the purpose of telling my story, I sincerely hope you can connect with me on a human level rather than just seeing another victim in the news. After all, we are all not so different from each other. We are born without knowing prejudice, hate or bias. Growing up, the first feeling we receive is tenderness. If we remember what love, laughter and compassion is, we can remain resilient, strong, and learn something along the way while navigating through difficult situations.

Resilience is not like a trampoline, where you are down one second and up the following. It is more like climbing a mountain without a map. It requires some investment, strength and help from individuals around you, and you will probably still encounter difficulties en route. Eventually though, you arrive at the top and glance back at how far you have come.

Now, this must be relatable to a lot of women readers here; when we talk about women's problems in life, half of them are because of the patriarchal and misogynistic mindset underlying our culture and society. Regardless of women's education, skills and abilities, our society fosters the perspective that women are always less than men; they are weaker, they cannot support themselves, and most importantly, they are nothing without men! We have been struggling and fighting with this view since historical times, yet there were women who managed to pave and clear their ways into the male-dominated world, and I admire them wholeheartedly. For instance, women like Jane Austen are an inspiration for me. I wish I could write like her so that my work could show the world how messed up people are towards women and actually make an impact through it. She outlines the expectations placed on women within her society through satire, and when she writes her characters, she shows these standards that were imposed on women and how they question them.

Even at that time, women were not treated as strong, intelligent, and equal to men. They were perceived as not being able to think and make decisions for themselves. They were put in boxes, expecting not to break any rules of society. Like her, I also want my readers to connect with circumstances similar to mine, which they may have faced or may still be facing right now in their lives.

In light of our race or nationality, the family culture is similarly incredible and starts comparably early. Young women have several areas of expectations in the family unit, including marriage, beauty and obedience. In many societies, women are expected to be answerable for things that men are not, and that's exactly what I faced. There is more pressure put on young girls and women to look and act in typical ways. Numerous Asian, Indian, Hispanic and Latino societies accept that young women (whether the youngest or the oldest) should take care of the men in the family. Time and time again, this culture shows as one of the biggest influences of our gender beliefs and gender roles—and seems to be ubiquitous across most races and ethnicities.

This is what I believe is the root cause of the abusive behavior of men. They have seen women taking care of them all their lives and them not doing anything in return, making them believe how women should be treated. You may have experienced this too. Where do these cultural beliefs come from? Likely, they were passed down to you by your parents or your relatives because that's what they believed in. These cultural inconsistencies of how we treat women send a message to young girls and boys, and then they act accordingly. The bottom line is that strong cultural and societal influences can impact your personality and the personalities of the women around you as well.

The expectations of marriage are the concluding standard that I stress. For the sake of economic stability, they are bound to stay and work through it, which in turn brings in the abusive factor in married life most of the time. So far as the abuse is concerned, the biggest irony is that whenever a victim speaks up about the physical or sexual abuse they face, they are perceived as "dramatic" or someone who has lost her family's dignity. This creates a sense of isolation, distrust and fear in the mind of a victim. It neglects and denies the tools needed to cope with stress and to learn new skills to become resilient, strong, and successful.

One of my goals for my readers to know in my story is that, through it, you can get an insight into what I faced and how I challenged it. We need to challenge these cultural expectations that hold us, women, accountable for things that men are generally not. We are capable of doing big things. We can be as successful as men can be.

CHAPTER 1: WOMEN LIKE US

For me, considering how kind of a rebel I am, being a woman was a tough job. But this also meant that I could do the job just as well. This made me believe that I am capable of doing it. No one can change my perspective otherwise. I have a firm belief that women are much more competent. Women in almost all modern populations live longer. And research shows that women generally live longer than men, and that is because women survive better than men. I believe that the main reason is that women are more able to cope with crisis situations than their counterpart. They have the ability to survive better under difficult circumstances, extending to crises such as famines, epidemics and slavery.[2]

Therefore, when it comes to longevity, surviving and coping with trauma, one gender comes out on top. Physical strength can be characterized in various ways. At this point, I was to learn that, underneath our skin, women bubble with a wellspring of power that even science still cannot seem to comprehend completely. We are born this way. Strength, toughness, or power—whatever it is called—this capacity for endurance breaks the stereotype in any society. The physically strong, muscular woman is a fantasy, a myth. We look at great sportswomen and athletes like they are supernatural creatures. Greek legend could hardly comprehend the Amazons, female warriors as incredible as men. They break the laws of nature. Now, we, the ordinary everyday women, may only have half the upper body strength of men. We may be six inches shorter. But we employ power, both emotional and intellectual. It's not in our bodies. It's not just a grown-up woman, baby girls are robust, and it's always a mystery. For some reason, I want to believe that girls may be getting an extra dose of survivability in the womb.

For all of this, my take is that it is to be appreciative when things are going great in life. In my opinion, the actual test is when we are grateful amid dire circumstances. My response to these situations is that not only will attitude of gratefulness help, but it is essential. Obviously, it is a difficult task, but in fact, it is exactly during crisis when we have to maintain a grateful perspective in life. And that would be my advice to all of you as well!

Chapter 2

Early Life

Antigua, Guatemala, is the largest colonial city in Latin America. It was the headquarters of the conquistadors from the southern part of Mexico to a part of Gran Colombia, the present-day Republic of Panama.

Three beautiful and mesmerizing volcanoes surround my town. My great grandfather Diego used to plant coffee, strawberries, figs, oranges, and all sorts of fruit trees on the outskirts of Volcán de Agua.

As a child, I was a happy kid who used to roam freely everywhere I could. My mother and my sisters had traditional Mayan Indian hair, jet black, straight and long, but my younger brother and I had curly hair. My mother had no idea how to handle my curls. She was constantly fighting to comb my hair and make it tidy, just for me to go out of her sight and let my hair loose.

My childhood was beautiful. It reminded me of all the good things of the past. I remember running around in November and December when children usually are off from school. I used to play, catch butterflies, cut branches and do every little thing to live in the moment and enjoy. I used to look for the little dangerous passages to challenge my little brother and myself. As soon as I could read, I tried to interpret poems, and loved them.

My mother had a record player which she let me use and I would play classical music, usually in the afternoons, and especially when it was raining. The music would bring melancholy as if it came from an unknown source in the past. I was convinced that I had lived another life. From when I was seven, I constantly recited to my mother the details of how I looked when I was a young woman in her late twenties. I described the clothes I wore, the color of my skin, my beautiful golden curls and how tall I was. But I was never able to see my face. I claimed to have been a teacher with authority, that got people to follow my commands. Looking back at my childhood, I can describe myself as perfectionist. I always kept myself clean and tidy and liked home to be in perfect order. I always wanted everybody to keep things nice after the housekeeper cleaned the house, and it would upset me when my family did not keep it that way.

I often said to mother that when I was big, people listened to me. My mother would get upset when I talked about my "other life." Upon asking her the reason, she told me that I was getting her a bit scared. She was

CHAPTER 2: EARLY LIFE

beginning to think I was possessed by spirits. Insisting they were only dreams, one day mom begged me to stop talking about my "past life". I stopped but never forgot the details, which until today are vivid in my mind. In my childhood, I was never fortunate enough to meet my paternal grandfather, as he died before I came into the world. I also don't remember meeting my paternal grandmother, but I know that she met me. My grandmother was not very fond of my mother. She never liked the idea of my father marrying a widow with three children, even though she was a widow too. When I was born, I had a remarkable resemblance to my father, but she always found something wrong with me. Her name was Carmen. When she first saw me, she told my dad that my legs were crooked, and I should undergo surgery immediately. I was about two months old at the time.

She did not like the idea of me not being perfect, as she thought her son was. My Dad was not even close to perfect but was a good dad to us five. He never treated my other three siblings any different than my younger brother and me. Him and Mom went through incredible sagas together. My grandmother Carmen wasn't right. My legs were not crooked, and I grew up to be a perfect runner and a basketball player.

I had tight relationship with my brothers. We got along well and respected each other. My mother was an excellent house manager and teacher. She always designated tasks to help us bond. Even though we always had to do our own chores, we also had to take care of each other. Everyone was responsible for washing their own uniforms, shining shoes the night before school, finishing homework, and helping the youngest to do theirs.

Growing up between two boys did not help when choosing my activities. I loved climbing trees, play marbles and all kinds of boy's games to the point where my mother worried for me. Sometimes I would be scruffy and dirty with scars on my legs from when I fell or tripped while running and competing with the dogs to see who could get on the other side of the block faster.

My mother would get upset, thinking that my legs would be ruined and scarred when I grow up. She would constantly ask me to be like my older sisters and act more like a lady. But I knew was never going to be like them because I was too different. As they were much older than me, they had formed a little clan; always doing things together and already into boys. Sometimes they would even go to parties with my mother because she was very young looking (and still is today) with fabulous skin. Thank you, mom, for my good genes.

She was sixteen when she got married, so practically a teenager when she had my two older sisters. I enjoyed the company of my brothers, the dogs, and my friends. After seeing my legs full of scars, my mother would apply a disinfectant with a distinctive orange color on my legs. She used to count all the scars to ensure I wouldn't get new ones. I used to raise my long socks to my knees so she could only count the visible scars.

CHAPTER 2: EARLY LIFE

I had several relatives living abroad, and often they came to our place to visit and spent time with us. They always asked about my siblings and the rest of the family. I remember my mother always speaking fondly about my siblings, except me. When my relatives ask for the "little girl", my mom will roll her eyes, disapproving of my behavior.

"Oh, Diana!" she would reply.

Was I a problem child or just different? My siblings used to fight just like any siblings do. But if mom scolded the troublemaker, I would jump in and try to stop her from dishing out punishment, even though I used to hit them in a fight, I disliked seeing someone else hurting them.

When I was little, I ran away three times. The first time I believe I was only two and a half years old. I took my cousin to the nearby park two blocks away. Everyone else was busy at home getting ready for a party. My cousin and I were of about same age. The police and firefighters were called to look for the two missing toddlers. All I remember is a lady who came to us and asked if we were hungry. I can't track down the exact details of the event, but my cousin and I ended up eating cookies and watching cartoons in her place.

After some time, the police, my mother, my aunt and other relatives found us. My cousin ran to her mom while I stayed in the cozy cushions on the floor watching cartoons. The policeman asked me, pointing at my mom, if I knew her. I answered in negative. **Poor mom, I cannot** imagine what she must have felt. Of course, I was taken home and mom installed safety locks on all doors. I don't think I was a troublemaker as in reality I didn't want to cause any trouble.

Another of my escapades was when I had been promised to "help" put flags on the front roof of the house to celebrate Independence Day. Guatemalans still do it every 15 September, although I'm not sure how independent we actually are. Mind you, in grammar school, we used to recite every day in order of importance, "Our country, our teachers and our parents" as the most important things in our lives. Since I was promised the adventure to the roof and was later denied, I got pretty disappointed. After crying for ten minutes and no one paying attention, I decided to walk away to a more deserving family. I was found the same day at 11 p.m. in my friend's place around the corner. When police questioned me about the issue, I simply said that I didn't want to live with my family anymore because they were unfair, to which my mom rightfully reacted by grabbing me by my ear and dragging me back home. That was when I started asking mother about my birth mother, because I could not accept her as my real Mom; we could never seem to understand each other. I was different, and knew home was somewhere else. I warned her to take me back to my real family. Mom, I said, the longer you wait, the more difficult it would be for you to get used to me being gone.

Usually, when you are in the middle of a crisis or are confused between reality and your emotions, you think about the outrage later. My mother said to me more than once that I would get a deserved lesson when I married and had children like yourself. When I got married, I first had two boys, but they both were good and caused me no trouble at all. I often thought about my mother proved wrong. Years later, I got my daughter. When she was ten, I thought about Mom again. I grabbed the phone and asked her to forgive me for all the times I had made her upset.

The year was 1970, and according to the letters we received, Dad was happy in New York and doing well at work. My mother was to follow him to the US, but my maternal grandmother became ill. Being the closest to her, my mother stayed behind to care for and organize her hospital treatments. After three years Grandma Francisca returned to heaven. Once again, Mom was ready to join Dad in New York; not with all of us, but the youngest first. Her plan was frustrated again by another sad event, marking her faith as wife and mother in an unprecedented manner.

The Civil War entered full swing. As far back as I can remember, helicopters flew over major towns, dropping little pieces of colorful paper. We would pick them up as if it was confetti. The papers read, "If you see someone strange, somebody who doesn't belong to your neighborhood, report them to the authorities."

The situation was awful and traumatic. I remember Mom running around to our neighbor's house with the only phone line in the block to call my older siblings after a bomb explosion to check if they were still alive. Military trucks loaded with **soldiers roaming the country**. I remember feeling intimidated and scared every time we got close to one of them. I clearly remember the disturbing smell of bodies decomposing in ditches along the road between Guatemala City, Port San Jose and Antigua. Several Catholic priests got murdered, and some were shot in front of their churches. Their only crime committed was attempting to protect innocent people fleeing persecution. In the highlands, indigenous communities got disseminated just for offering water or food to passing strangers, who happened to be members of the revolutionary movement.

In 1996, after 36 years of civil war, the peace accord was **finally agreed. The loss** of life was unprecedented, with about 200,000 civilians dead. Many sons, daughters, fathers, mothers, and children remain missing with no grave to deposit a flower and chant a prayer. I cry as I remember the sadness of my country during such a dark period. Guatemala, and other Central American countries, got set back at least 50 years. Progress stalled and education still not compulsory. Remember, where there is knowledge, there is awareness, and uneducated **populations don't question governments**. Until today, the land of the "Eternal Spring" is infested with corruption, poverty, and crime. It is a must to teach world history in school. Societies everywhere need to learn not to make the same mistakes.

CHAPTER 2: EARLY LIFE

It's a fact that money will not make polluted fields return to be fertile or contaminated water turn pure. The first university students who rebelled against the injustice at the begging of the civil war fought for land, food and freedom. I have experienced in two monumental, life-changing episodes that money has proven to weigh more than justice.

For the full background on the facts of the Guatemalan Civil War, I would strongly recommend reading *Bitter Fruit: The Untold Story of the American Coup in Guatemala*[3] by Stephen C. Schlesinger. It is one of the best books that offers accurate details about the war. For the basics of why Latin American countries are no longer the superpowers they once were, I would recommend *Open Veins of Latin America*[4] by Eduardo Galeano.

Guatemala is a volcanic region with thirty-five volcanoes in a small country. In 1976, a devastating earthquake struck the country killing about 23,000 people, leaving 76,000 injured out of a population of 7 million.

The situation continued to worsen as we were growing up. Universities were mostly shut down during that time, and young people attending the National Conservatory to listen to professionals in their field would get kidnapped on their way out of the venue. We saw white jeeps with no license plates kidnapping high schoolers, some my peers. We ran like sheep and hid in terror. We later found out the military were attempting to threaten, scare, and discourage anyone thinking or trying to pursue higher education. So yes, naturally, I became part of several revolutionary's student groups. In our high school, we had several leaders. We were scared, but it was awful to not do anything about it.

Bombs were detonated in shopping centers, schools, and buses. Innocent people were getting killed, and the survivors had no clue why they were the target of a genocide. It was clear that more than power, it was about control, such applied by external manipulation over a small country who wanted to succeed, feed and get fed from their land. Back in the 50s, Guatemala was self-sufficient, and that was the problem; we were independent, and flourishing.

I got involved with student revolutionaries, trying to make a change, trying to get what we yearned for; that is, education to fill the gaps. So, we protested, marched in the streets and extract information about the whereabouts of all the bodies of the children who were kidnapped. Where were our friends? Where were all the high schoolers taken away in the unidentified white jeeps?

It was painful waking up to the news that the lifeless bodies of kidnapped students getting dumped near their high schools. Their bodies showed evidence of torture and rape. Some of our martyrs were never located. At one point, my parents became concerned about my safety and decided it was time for me to leave the country to get further education. They flew me to New York to live with my father. I had to leave behind my siblings, my mother, the rest of my relatives, good friends, and fellow rebels and revolutionaries' students. I felt like a coward; sad and impotent for doing so. It was discouraging when the realization hit me that I was a grain of sand on a vast beach, and there was not much I could achieve. I was tiny, fighting against an enormous monster swallowing all in its path. I still fill angry when remembering those times.

Then, I went to New York but promised to return wiser. My plan then formulated into attaining better education, building myself a solid career, and then finding a strong and impactful voice that would give me the power to be heard far and wide. I wanted to dedicate my life to my people, my family and all those who suffered unjustly. And so there I was inching closer to New York. It was November, and the cold of Winter was waiting for me. The tops of buildings grazing the heavens put me in an awe I had never known before.

Chapter 3

My Family

There is a cliché that says family is one of the greatest gifts of God. I believe at some point, it is true. We all must know that it is a privilege to belong to a bunch of people who, at some point in life, can be called *yours*.

As for me, I have had majorly different dynamics with all of my family members. This happens—our relationship varies with each one of them. You must have too.

For example, I was very close to my maternal grandmother, Francisca. I have plenty of fond memories of her. She was the one who took me to kindergarten on my first day. Grandma prepared me for the big day, running my bath in the morning with warm water. In the sunny side of the garden next to a fig tree; she applied baby cologne. Grandma reassured me that she would be at the same door to collect me and promised a treat if I didn't cry.

I loved my grandmother Francisca. It was with her that I learned about coffee and influenced my obsession with it to this day. Every afternoon, around 4 p.m., she would call me for coffee time. We used to chat for endless hours. I just cannot imagine what type of conversations we had. What type of conversation would you have with a five-year-old? She always had plenty of things to say. I think the main reason I am now capable of knowing practical things about life is because of her. That's what happens when you spend time with the elders in your home. Their experiences make you learn a lot about life. I remember my mother feeling jealous about my coffee time gatherings. But my grandma and I didn't care. We continued our routine unless she was in the hospital or visiting relatives in another town. When I was in Hong Kong, I became a coffee connoisseur and treasured every single cup of coffee I drank, and more often than not, I remember my coffee time with grandma.

In some Central American countries, the school year ends in October, leaving November and December to celebrate with family, year-end festivals and holidays. The beginning of November is marked by the Day of the Dead and December starts with the burning of the devil followed by Christmas and New Year. In my childhood years, children didn't have many choices for where to spend their free time except for home or in the street, playing with each other, with neighbors and taking care from the oldest to the youngest.

CHAPTER 3: MY FAMILY

I remember playing in the street with neighborhood dogs and raising them too. My friends were mostly boys. I don't know why but I found that I got along better with them. Maybe because I grew up between two brothers; my eldest was one of my most significant mentors in my life. It felt very natural for me to spend time with them and their friends.

While we used to go out to play, my mother always had my older brother watching after me and just like that, I was obliged to take care of my younger brother as well. We used to compete. I used to have so much fun with my younger brother. I became the leader of his group of friends and was in charge of organizing games and dangerous places to climb or explore. I loved playing all those games, which are socially constructed for boys. My rebellious personality did not conform with gender limitations, making my childhood free and very colorful.

At the same time, I had this element of romanticism deeply rooted in me; I loved to read poems and listening to classical music. One sunny afternoon, I remember wearing my pale-yellow dress, my curls all over the place, accompanied with a small poetry book on hand—the poem was "The Girl of Guatemala." It is a sad poem about a wealthy girl who falls in love with the Cuban poet and philosopher, Jose Martí.[5] He promised to return to her, but when he returned, he was already married. She died; she died of love. Then suddenly I stop to think about it—this is nonsense! Nobody dies out of love. I am not going to suffer out of love. I am not going to die out of love. I left the book and went to play with my friends. Little did I know, that in the future I would become so acquainted with the deadly pain of love.

I can now relate to the poem. Deep inside, I feel as if a piece of my heart broke and would never be the same. I read an article about how scientists discovered that the heart has a memory as well as the brain.[6] It is true. Hearts do have memory.[7] My ex-husband's cruelty and betrayal left me traumatized. I also believe my heart experienced the pain. After all, trauma is not what happens to you: it's what happens inside you. When painful memories recur, my heart tightens as if trying to hide from the truth. The poem I read as a child is recurring in my mind—*The Girl of Guatemala*. The same one I discarded, thinking that such a thing never happened in real life, and here I was facing suffocating pain I could not explain. But peace will help, and love mends almost everything. So, wait patiently, my dear heart, together we will overcome.

The Girl of Guatemala

At a wing's shade;
to tell this tale in bloom:
about the girl from Guatemala,
the girl who died of love.

The flowers were made of lilies
and mignonette ornaments,
and jasmine: we buried her in a silk casket...

She gave to the forgetful
a scented sachet.
he came back, came back married;
she died of love.

She was carried in a procession
by bishops and ambassadors;
the town followed behind in batches,
all carrying flowers...

She, wanted to see him again,
stepped out to the balcony;
he came back with his wife,
she died of love.

Like red hot bronze,
was the farewell kiss,
it was her forehead, the forehead
that I have loved most in my life!...

She went into the river at dusk,
the doctor pulled her out dead;
some say she died from cold,
I know she died of love.

There, on the frozen vault
they placed he on two benches;
I kissed her cold hand.
I kissed her white shoes.

Quietly, when dusk came,
the undertaker called me;
I have never seen again
the one who died of love.

José Martí

Chapter 4

The House

Where do you see your life in three, seven or even ten years? Some of our dreams feed from our thoughts, planning and future goals we wish to accomplish. Suppose we pour enough passion and interest into those dreams. Then, creativity unleashes, and limitations cease—specifics about how and when become somehow irrelevant. I am a dreamer, and the more I think about my dreams, the more excited I get. One of the most precious dreams was having a house with gardens inundated with orchids and bougainvillea, waking up to the fuss of colibris (hummingbirds) collecting nectar. I dream of love and remain faithful to the promise that one day I will return to the motherland.

This long-held promise to myself was eventually realized, and the first step began with the search for a house. With a modest budget and vast enthusiasm, the quest began. For ten years grew stronger, dragging along family and many plans for the future. There were a few requirements to finding the perfect place, firstly, it had to be an original building close to foot traffic and commerce. An option of a new building did not satisfy the desire to stay in character with the city's rich history and architecture.

The other requirements pertained to commercial development. Michael and I dreamt of possibilities where we could include family and employ locals—especially single mothers—and contribute to the local economy.

Despite our friends in New York advising us not to invest in a country known for its high crime rate, frequent earthquakes and volcanic spews, we focused on weaving dreams of waking up surrounded by the beauty of volcanoes, eating freshly grown food, fresh mountain air far from pollution, and doing good for the local community whilst earning a living ourselves.

Finally in 2008 while my family and I were visiting relatives in Guatemala, a call from an unknown estate agent reached us. He was inviting us to view a property recently added on the market. My daughter and husband were hungry, and we almost didn't attend. Michael was always a part of the big decisions, but I insisted on seeing the property. I requested the hungry pair ten minutes to inspect. If it wasn't to our liking, we could leave immediately. Clambering onto a tuk-tuk moments later, we made our way down the cobblestone streets, bouncing our way toward the given address.

The owner, a foreign man named Roy, had inherited the property from his father. Roy had other properties abroad and no desire to spend time in Guatemala. After over ten years of neglect, the property was in a grave state of disrepair with a leaking roof, moldy walls, dilapidated old pool, broken floors from previous seismic activity, and ancient plumbing. But it was of a good size, with a few original walls from the early 50s, the price was right and in a good location. Roy told us he had an agreed sale, but the buyer did not attend the final meeting. So he contacted a real estate agent with a few days to spare before his departing flight.

Michael was always in charge of the family investments and significant decisions, so with the help of an English-speaking lawyer, an anonymous association came to be. Roy deposited the asset into Avenida Sur S.A., and as far as I understand, we never received a tangible property but rather shares, which Roy also held over the property. If you find these archaic terms strange—you are not alone. I left Guatemala when I was a girl, so certain details and conditions were unfamiliar and confusing for me too. Michael had chosen how to manage our affairs with the local lawyer and what was best for us at the time. I had to search independently and understand what some terms meant. In essence, an Anonimus Association or an (S.A.) Sociedad Anónima in Spanish is similar to a Limited Company (Ltd) or Corporation (Corp). The judiciary department most frequently grants the first two because they are the most widely used in Latin America's corporate world. What differentiates an S.A. from the rest is the small amount of capital needed. It also serves well when the number of investors is small. Like in many other countries, company records are for public viewing. Unfortunately, technological advances have not helped when in the wrong hands. Organized crime with bands of kidnappers and extortionists can also easily find names and addresses of company owners and investors, putting their safety at risk. So, for small companies and start-ups, forming an S.A. is the best choice for personal security as it is only under such circumstances that their details remain sealed from public view.

A dream was materializing and plans to add more assets would soon come. The celebration of finding a suitable property did not last long. Michael announced that we had to move from New York to London, and the construction had not even started. Finding a good architect and filing for renovation permits was a bit of a nightmare as the city of Antigua is a UNESCO World Heritage Site. A guardian was needed to caretake the dilapidated place, ensuring no passage to squatters.

The renovation itself was an absolute nightmare. I had learned the hard way when I oversaw construction projects from our previous two properties in New York. Another story dignified for a separate book! When Michael wants something, everyone else become his minions to achieve his desires. So, when we noticed the lack of diligence from the architect overseeing the renovation, I often had to drop everything in London, leave my child with the nanny and fly to Guatemala to check on the refurbishment.

We also had several of my family members involved in overseeing the renovation. Two of my cousins paid frequent visits to the site, and another began to full-time keep

CHAPTER 4: THE HOUSE

track of the quantity and quality of materials bought and used. Primarily in charge was my older sister, who was keen on being part of whichever business we were going to launch. She is older than I am and understandably concerned about her and her son's future. Unfortunately, in Guatemala and most Latin American countries, once a person reaches a certain age, it's tough to gain employment. Flory worked for thirty years with the same employer. She had seen her bosses' three sons grow up and often helped with homework when they came to the office after school. When Flory's boss and business owner passed, her three sons took over. They made many changes and asked my sister to sign a new work contract. Little did she know that the intention behind the three new owners was to strip her of thirty years of retirement benefits paid by the employer, not the government. She fought back, but two of the three owners were lawyers, and legal costs were eating her savings. When the new owners began to intimidate her, she stopped the process, and thirty years in retirement funds went out the window. For Michael and me, Flory was an obvious choice as the first of our future partners. As Michael put it, she was competent, keen to help, trustworthy and loyal.

After the renovation began, we went through several months of tumultuous incidents. But the real problems started about eighteen months into the renovation. The architect would routinely not show up at the site; the engineer's specified materials were replaced by inferior alternatives. The workers stopped receiving their pay, and in the end he vanished altogether!

My older sister slept on the property countless nights in unsuitable conditions to protect it from break-ins. A cousin would also begin surveillance, as we feared unpaid workers would retaliate. Without consideration, Michael would call our family in Guatemala asking for help. In his tantrums, he would scream at them saying that they were closer to the property and therefore needed to do more to help.

As the budget tightened, all the laborers started walking out. I flew back to Antigua immediately and landed without knowing how to fix the mountain of problems and unfinished work on the abandoned construction site.

Firstly, I went to the construction supply company and asked if they knew laborers looking for work. But the word was out; no one wanted to return to a work site that did not pay. From my cousin, I learned the names of the companies that delivered the construction materials. I embarked on a tour to visit almost all of them until an electrical supply distributor heard the real story and referred me to an electrician looking for work. Then feeling guilty and ashamed for something the architect had done, I put a sign on the door. I prayed for builders seeking employment to see it, "Construction workers needed, get paid daily, landlord hiring." I managed to recruit a few new workers after I explained the issues I faced with the architect; these workers helped me by calling colleagues familiar with the site.

I was in a tough spot and had to rely on these workers to get the necessary plumbing and electricity up and running before the construction permit expired. A

CHAPTER 4: THE HOUSE

prohibition of moving debris out of the house would become effective; several water leaks destroyed previous floor tiles in communal areas and had to get replaced. I must have spent at least three months onsite. There were workers taking day and night shifts. I cried in despair whenever an electrical cable in the wall was found dead, and walls had to get opened to resolve the problem—the same with water pipes when water began to emerge on the floor and walls. After excavating, we discovered waterpipes that were not sealed or adequately joined. My sisters' and my tears permeated the floors and walls of the property until all essential work culminated. It was evident that sister Flory had what it took to help us build a successful business. In 2013 Flory became a second shareholder of the company.

A few weeks had passed and around April 2014, Michael announced that we had to move to Hong Kong. Planning for a business in Guatemala was once again postponed for about six weeks and shortly after we arrived in South Asia, I became president of the Spanish-Speaking Women's Association of Hong Kong; helping several charities and interacting with locals led me to roam the main island and its new territories. I learned about the many specialty coffee houses and barista champions searching for their next exotic coffee to showcase.

It became apparent to me which product to source from Guatemala. A country with thirty-five volcanoes, two hundred microclimates and a niche market which prioritizes high quality over quantity with its organic raw coffee beans. I put on my thinking hat and began researching how to achieve importing coffee to Hong Kong from Guatemala. Taking classes and learning when and how to proceed as a buyer was arduous. Learning logistics applicable to small buyers like myself was another big task as not many retailers like to deal with small businesses. Whenever I could, I would travel to Guatemala to visit relatives and my elderly mother; combining it also with my pursuit of local micro-coffee growers. I would also visit coffee houses and ask them about their suppliers. I also became familiar with barista champions and the youngest coffee taster in the world, Mr. Jorge De Leon, who steered me in the right direction on how and where to source the best raw coffee beans.[8]

As I came to learn, opening a business in Hong Kong was complex, but in mid-2016, I finally founded a company in Hong Kong to import coffee. The enthusiasm was great. Despite not having any stock in the warehouse, I already had one customer interested in buying my Guatemalan brown gold. My sister helped a great deal when we began buying. She organized deliveries and made the property she helped me renovate suitable to store the coffee before shipment. Green coffee grain is delicate and needed special handling, so with the help of a carpenter, Flory created a platform for the coffee bags to rest whilst air passed underneath to allow the grain to breathe, preventing the humidity from accumulating.

My sister and I interacted with small-scale growers. We learned about the troubles ANACAFE—The National Coffee Association—gave them when sourcing their export licenses and other permits. Flory and I helped several farmers complete appropriate forms and sometimes drove them to the city to make their applications while we waited alongside them. ANACAFE is the governmental entity in charge of handling coffee production and distribution licenses. There is much to say about ANACAFE and very little regarding positive experiences when dealing with them. Small coffee growers often suffer discrimination and receive little help in their attempts to certify the quality of their coffee beans.

After much toil, my dreams and hopes for the coffee business crashed like the pyroclastic rocks that pummel down to earth after a volcanic eruption. In 2017 after discovering my ex-husband's affair, he stopped our daughter and me from traveling. I needed more stock and decided to buy remotely with the help of my sister. Unfortunately, shipping became an ordeal and expensive because the quantity ordered diminished. I tried relentlessly to keep the business running, but when Michael left our daughter and me behind in Hong Kong and moved to London, the money I received diminished and was limited. He was no longer interested in escaping to the land of Eternal Spring and helping a local community, forgetting also of the promises made to my sister. The dream began to crumble, and in a way, me with it.

Chapter 5

Bittersweet

Sometimes I felt incapable of recounting certain events, but in this chapter, I will pen down the bittersweet of my travel journey during the relevant period of this story.

Painful memories, voices, melodies and smells trigger anxiety attacks. I can't be in an elevator with men dressed in suits. I feel as if my ex-husband is ready to jump out from behind and grab my neck.

Avoiding it all costs the day before, I started the next day with a run and following that retreated to the living room, putting on the soothing tones of Bach to accompany me. Only then could I begin to jot down and detail the bittersweet memories that ensued.

Michael, the children, and I, travelled to many places around the world. Unfortunately, most are bad memories. I remember Michael's tantrums when something was not the way he wanted. For example, when we went skiing, he would complain about paying for the lift passes to the mountain. In his eyes, the boys were wasting his money because they didn't use as many hours as they could while the lifts were open. Not to mention on other trips which would usually include an itinerary of Michael's places of interest; which if met with any opposition we'd all be rebuked and called ignorant.

It breaks my heart to think about all the times that we could have been happy but weren't. Instead, we were more often than not upset with each other. The children used to get upset with me because I mostly tried to appease him. I wanted him to be my husband, but I couldn't have one. Instead, I had to raise him along with the other three children. In the end, I got tired of being his mother. If you are experiencing a similar situation, please stop! Children grow up and leave you, precisely what your man-child will do. In her own words, my mother-in-law told me so about Michael's father, and it seemed as if Michael never appreciated his mother's suffering by behaving like his father.

Michael's fights with the children were my fights. Whenever he used to push them to give more at school, I would jump in, trying to set balance. My ex-husband was obsessed with the children getting into higher and more challenging subjects or levels. They used to cry and moan when Michael attempted to "help" with their homework. He is a mathematician and insisted that complex assignments were "simple" and couldn't understand how his children did not get it. Sometimes he would slap them, and push them around, especially the two boys. I would

CHAPTER 5: BITTERSWEET

intervene and get Michael to divert his anger on me instead. He harmed their mental wellbeing. Michael is guilty of our children's traumas and nightmares which until this day lurk in the back of their minds during sad, disappointing days. Sadly enough, the children only remembered the fights, but not the reason for my involvement. As a mother my duty was to defend and protect them and feel proud of how I handled it all.

When I met Michael, he was an unstable Class A drug user, buried in student loans and unpaid electric and phone bills. I worked hard to get him into Narcotics Anonymous. Still, as it turns out, he seemed to need a vice, so he became a smoker and following that a functional alcoholic. I should have known that my path to being the mother who rejected him for lack of patience and direction would rest on my shoulders for decades to come.

I had so little, but money management was my strength; by the time we married, I already had two credit cards and loan approvals of up to $20,000 USD. Because of my credit and savings, Michael could afford his first ever brand-new car. Unfortunately, no matter how much money comes into Michael's hands, he will burn it as if there is no tomorrow. His luxurious traveling taste is an addiction that has often left him in debt and waiting for the next paycheck. The irony that he became the Chief Financial Officer for three companies blows my mind.

I helped Michael in every way I could. By observing his shortcomings, I noticed that he had trouble making friends. On the contrary, the element of human interaction for me came more easily and was something that gave me great joy. I often made the introduction to most of Michael's acquaintances and friends in London and Hong Kong. Later, you will understand why I am mentioning them in this chapter.

When choosing my friends, I don't care about their business, title, political or social status, or what they do for a living. Instead, I gravitate towards their character, life experiences and good natures; which can be difficult to find, but not impossible. My first rule is give your full attention to the other person when speaking, not so you can reply, but so you can empathize. Second, remember that we all crave attention, compassion and empathy. Give these out in buckets. Third, friends are the family you choose to have. So, through the years, I managed to accumulate a good set of acquaintances and friends. Some of those friends helped me a great deal during my darkest moments in 2017 and still today. I had shoulders to cry on, compassionate words that brought me peace, a spare sofa when I had no place to sleep and sometimes even money to meet my most basic needs.

Mercedes' Birthday

My baby girl was born in July 2000. We named her Diana-Mercedes. The weight of the name of a goddess of the hunters, childbirth, light, moon and courage had served me well in life; I thought it would help my little girl navigate hers with courage. Mercedes is my mother's name and symbolizes kindness. So, in hopes of strengthening the name, I chose to hyphenate them to protect her with the compassion denoted in the name Mercedes; from Latin origin meaning "mercies," the plural of mercy and used in reference to the Virgin Mary, Santa Maria, the last Mercedes, or Lady of Mercy. On a literary theme, it was also the name of the last lover of Edmund Dante's, the Count of Monte Cristo.

In 2015, Mercedes reached her 15th birthday. In Latin America, celebrating the Sweet Fifteen or Quinceañera (as it is called in Spanish) is the traditional way families present their sons and daughters to society. It is a big celebration to give grace to the child surviving diseases during early age and reaching the second of four significant stages of life: childhood, adolescence, adulthood, and elder or wisdom period.

During that time, we were living in Hong Kong. I began planning the event and, with great joy, took care of every single detail of the event from abroad. Mercedes and I had fun thinking about dress colors, style, lengths, shoes, makeup, and all sorts of girly things for the party. The celebration was to take place in Antigua, Guatemala, so most of our elderly relatives could attend. The list of guests became long and diverse. Friends and family began planning their trip. I had formed a tight friendship with two school friends during my undergraduate studies. A woman named Lina was taking English as a second language in a part-time program in the same college. Back in the early nineties, she was already getting through the first of three divorces. One of the girls in the group introduced Lina to us to help support her during the divorce.

For over twenty-five years, I cultivated a relationship with Lina. She and her family were therefore also invited to the Quinceañera, including her husband Bryan and their child who was about seven years old at the time. As an extra consideration, we decided they could stay in the house with the rest of our immediate family and use the help of the full-time housekeeper so they could enjoy more of the party. Meanwhile, the rest of the guests and family stayed in a hotel nearby within walking distance of the venue.

The birthday celebration was a success. Mercedes looked radiant with happiness. There were violins, belly dancing, choreography, competitions, the white tablecloths kissed the floors in reverence to the event. An assortment of pink and aquamarine flowers adorned tables and walkways. The Quinceañera walked from table to table, hugging friends and relatives; I saw her dancing with her father and, the grand prize was to see her shine. That Thursday evening, a glorious sunset adorned the skies with orange, red and golden tones. When the party ended, we all had laughed, ate and drank too much. Tired from lack of sleep from jetlag and the final arrangements, I longed to jump into bed. We all went to sleep past midnight.

At three o'clock in the morning, Lina's husband knocked on my bedroom door, startled and scared, thinking perhaps it was an earthquake. I answered the door. He seemed worried and asked me for his wife and if I knew where she was.

I half asleep replied, "She is in the bedroom with you."

CHAPTER 5: BITTERSWEET

He said, "No, she's not."

Thinking about a stomach virus, I said, "Maybe she is ill."

I turned on the bedroom lights to wake up my husband, but he wasn't there either. I thought that maybe I was too tired and did not hear Lina's knocking, seeking for help. I asked Bryan to look by the pool area and guardian quarters. I knew the house in the dark and headed to the living room, kitchen and breakfast area. The only place left was the mezzanine where the home office was. There, I found Lina completely drunk, passed out on the couch, with her legs wide open. Michael was sitting close to her next to the desk, half-drunk with a bottle of rum almost empty. I was shocked and could not understand what I was witnessing.

"Michael!" I said, "If you wanted to drink, you could have asked my brothers, cousins or any other male guest to accompany you for a drink. It is embarrassing...Lina's husband is looking for her!"

I called upon Bryan, directed him to go up to the mezzanine. He too, was embarrassed, and upset. Our talking woke up Lina, and she ejected herself from the sofa, repeating, "Nothing happened! Nothing happened…"

I could not understand what she meant. I would have never imagined close to two years in the future what I would hear from my husband's lips about what took place that night. I went to bed crying with my husband next to me, mocking me for having made a scene. For the two remaining days, until all guests went home, I managed to keep face. But inside, I was in pain and full of shame.

My heart aches when I remember the details of what I just shared. I cry for the innocence stolen from our daughter because she learned to suffer from a broken heart even before having her first love. For the two marriages that got destroyed in such a drastic and vicious way; for our parents and relatives who tried to console us but couldn't, and for learning to mourn a person who is alive. Please don't steal, don't cheat, don't kill. Karma does take care of those who cause harm.

Texas

Our college group tries to organize yearly reunions. Almost three decades have passed since we shared our student life in New York City. We still laugh uncontrollably when remembering our silly subversive thoughts and the ideas we had to take over the world. Sometimes we included Lina in our trips. In January 2016, it was Lina who proposed a reunion. Of all places, she insisted on Texas. The other three friends and I were not keen to travel there. But Edith, the girl who introduced Lina to our group, pointed out that since Lina was constantly complaining about not having money, perhaps we should be more accommodating to her needs. I immediately sympathized with the idea because not long ago, Lina had asked me for money. She continued to carry a student loan of $80,000 USD and had pitched me for a "loan", but it was too much money and I couldn't help her anymore.

It was about time for her to grow up and take care of her messy life. Unfortunately, one of the girls decided not to join the trip to Dallas, Texas. Edith and I decided to go, and I invited my friend Patty, who lived in Sarasota, Florida. Taking advantage of my proximity to Guatemala, I also arranged a business trip to visit coffee growers to perform coffee sampling before shipping to Hong Kong.

A lot of strange things took place during our trip. Firstly, Lina insisted we stay an extra day near Dallas to visit and stay in her home. It was uncomfortable how she constantly mentioned not sleeping with her husband. The couple shared a child, bought a house, and seemed happy when we stayed in their place. Her husband Bryan was a polite man; worked as lawyer and had served the US armed forces or the Marines. An overall pleasant person. The other girls and I could not pinpoint the problem. Lina insisted that the relationship was a disaster. I was anxious to get going with our road trip, but Lina insisted on celebrating my birthday in her house. We finally sat and drafted our plans for our drive to San Antonio. At the last minute, she refused to drive us in her car. We had to shuffle around who would drive, who had a driver's license and where to get the car.

After seeing us struggling at the rental car place, Lina insisted on doing the driving. From the start of the trip, she began driving erratically, swerving in the road as if she was drunk and constantly looking through the rearview mirror to see the terror in Patty's and my face. Edith, sitting in the front next to Lina, asked several times what was wrong.

"I don't mind driving," Edith said. But Lina continued to hug the steering wheel for the whole trip.

After four hours of driving, we finally arrived in San Antonio. In the evening, we got dressed up and planned to listen to music and have dinner somewhere nice. Lina insisted that she wanted to check a place recommended to her. When we arrived at the bar, it was a trashy place, full of cowboys drinking and asking us to sit on their lap. It was scary; I told the girls that they had the choice of staying but that I was going back to the hotel. Neither Patty nor Edith wanted to stay either, so we had to drag Lina out of the bar. One of the girls mentioned the rotating restaurant in Tower of the Americas. Without a reservation, we walked into the tower and managed to get a nice dinner and laugh about the whole ordeal. Lina would constantly tell me that I looked like a beggar because everything looked good on me, no matter what I threw on my body. She asked a lot of questions about my sex life with my husband and other personal questions about Michael. I was put off by her attitude and asked her to stop her nonsense.

Lina's conversation got more deranged when she was drunk. At one point, she narrated details of working as a psychologist for abused young children—patients of hers, confidential things that she should never have been used as topics of conversation. One case, in particular, got stuck in my mind as shocking and perverse. It was about a little girl in Texas whose mother was a drug addict and had given her little girl to her boyfriend to use as a sex toy. The man would pin the child in an "X" shape to the wall, leave her sometimes for hours, then return to molest her again. What gave me shivers running down my spine was when

CHAPTER 5: BITTERSWEET

Lina confirmed going home and feeling aroused by the little girl's narrations and asking her husband to sexually tease her and leave her for a while before coming back to ejaculate. The deranged woman would complain that her husband was useless and impotent for not wanting to partake in the game. She called herself an "unlucky woman" because every man she married became impotent. Once over drinks, Lina stated that perhaps she was the only woman who liked sex more than men.

We laughed at her, thinking she was the picture in the dictionary when it came to "exaggeration." I don't know what her real story was, and in reality, I am not sure I ever met her authentic self. In May 2017, I found out how my husband and Lina cooperated in arranging the trip in preparation for their path of deception. The visit to her house in 2016 was all part of her well thought evil plan; she wanted her husband to see us together as friends. For me to tell Michael about her suffering and troubled marriage, helping to remove any guilt from Michael's mind when the time came to take Bryan's wife. One thing is for sure, she was never my friend. All the years of her nonsense eventually led to destruction and almost a death in my family.

"Any friend that turns into enemy has been hating since day one."[9]

Going back to 2016, I remember Michael planning our last big trip together, at least for a while. Soon our daughter Mercedes would be finishing high school. Her remaining holidays for 2017 designated to perform university tours, final International Baccalaureate exams and admission applications. We chose to visit the Golden Triangle and Rajasthan in India for December 2016, along with our German-Guatemalan friends under similar circumstances with their son one year older than our daughter. The trip was a dream come true, and I was extremely excited about finally visiting India.

August the same year, while picking up a heavy bag of groceries, I tore my right rotator cuff. The pain of tearing a tendon is difficult to bear. I lasted almost three months with the pain because of an early misdiagnosis. Alarms rang when I became feverish, resulting in emergency surgery. I had no idea that Michael had a trip planned to the United States. I needed a significant other with me at the hospital, and Michael had decided to go on with his travel plans. My good friend Yunani and her husband Javier offered to help me. The sweet couple were with me until it was time to be wheeled to the theatre room.

I remember having this terrible sadness in me, and suddenly, I had an anxiety attack and was shaking and crying uncontrollably, to the point where the nurses had to pull me out of the operating room. The anesthesiologist stayed with me in the hallway. I want to believe he was an angel who came to my aid. In a soft, caring voice, he told me that it was understandable if I was scared and asked me not to cry because I had the best surgeon in the hospital. He also asked if I was Christian or a believer because he wanted to pray for me. He held my hand and quietly prayed. I felt a warm feeling and saw a soft light that began

CHAPTER 5: BITTERSWEET

from the top of my head and rested on my shoulder, and then peace descended on me. A moment later, I felt ready to return to the operating room.

When our trip to India began, I was still recovering and shocked to learn that majority of the route would be over land, in rough terrain and inside an uncomfortable vehicle for eight people. Somehow, we ended up with an extra man in the car, in what was an already tight space. When we asked our driver, he replied that his friend needed a ride; I don't think there was much we could do except reluctantly accept the stranger onboard. The road trip was highly uncomfortable as my back and shoulder were constantly in pain. Michael would roll his eyes every time I proposed a stop to stretch my legs. I could feel something was wrong with him because he usually put on a façade in front of friends, but this time his behavior was rude to all in the group.

Some days there were seven or eight hours of driving. There was however always a castle waiting for us to stay in each of the cities we visited. We would have morning and afternoon activities. But Michael always managed to disappear in the afternoon and reappeared for dinner. Several times, he created chaos in our itinerary because he wanted to return to the hotel. The traffic of Mumbai is a nightmare during peak hours, but the poor tour guide would turn himself in a pretzel to fulfil Michael's requirements. I also noticed the peculiarity of Michael having an alarm set every day around the same time. Still, no evil crossed my mind at that time. Eyes that don't see, heart that doesn't feel. Michael became very mean and cruel during the trip. And the saddest part is that he involved our daughter in his antagonistic games.

New Year's festivities were upon us. The hotel planned a lovely celebration in their gardens facing Lake Pichola in Udaipur. The entire hotel was in a festive mood, except Michael. Ladies were to choose a sari from a vast display provided by the hotel and achkan for the gents. When the time came to collect our attire, Michael had convinced our daughter that it was pathetic to dress up for the night. Mercedes became hostile and told me that her dad said not to dress up with a sari because she would look like a fool. It saddens me that a grown man dragged our child into his dirty mental games. Our daughter trusted him, and he was a fraud. In the hope of encouraging Mercedes to wear a sari, I decided to collect mine. The color was fuchsia with golden trim. The psychology of the color fosters a sense of confidence and passion, similar to the color red. It suited my mood.

It was almost 8 p.m., I asked Michael and Mercedes if they were ready for picture taking, they laughed and proceeded to ignore me. When I got to the designated area, I felt out of place; while small groups of families and friends waited for their picture to get taken, I was alone; kept face, and when my turn came, I sat in a gorgeous silver throne-like chair and smiled. Michael and Mercedes finally joined the party, they were the only ones wearing regular clothes. When it was time to say goodbye to 2016, we received flying lanterns to release at midnight. Our family tradition is to ask for a wish; I looked at Michael, kissed him, and wished us well, health, happiness, a good job for him, and success for our children. I'm not sure what Michael wished for, but our relationship and family was definitely not on his mind at that time. So, I say to you my friends, it is easy to get divorced, and it is better to speak or even to walk away, but deception and cheating will only bring all the parties involved pain, chaos and a dark cloud that will follow you for a long time.

Chapter 6

Should I Stay?

The subsequent chapter is a set of memories from my recent past. I try to keep them locked in the very back of my mind. Yet, I know they are there, and they haunt me even when ignored. The pain turned into memories in a mist-like shape. I feel it next to me on sunny, cloudy or rainy days. It's mute but talks and moves next to me, but cannot walk. When the light reflects on it, it blinds me, and when it is dark, it sometimes consumes me.

These memories are the very reason I faithfully gave myself to meditation. Calming one's mind is quite challenging until you get to the point of understanding who is truly in control. Even the tiniest amount of learning about the ancient practice helped me block some harmful echoes of the past. I try to keep positive and remember there's always a lesson to be learned and an opportunity to evolve into a better person. If not for these experiences, I wouldn't have the opportunity to expose the injustices in my legal case. I aim to help other people going through similar situations and to expose the lack of accountability among members of a few legal firms and the Central Family Court of England.

I have been shuffling court documents for almost four years in a row. I witnessed my ex-husband's statements infested with perjury, lies and forgery throughout this period. It is torture, capable of destroying anyone's mental health and triggering a nervous breakdown. Yet, I diligently continued to fight despite unthinkable obstacles. I invite you to bear witness to my account, as impossible as it may sound: "Silence is a bad companion and enemy of justice."

I feel blessed to have been born with several qualities that helped me to navigate my path in this world; without a bit of obstinance, radical thinking and being a dreamer, I wouldn't have gone far. I also discovered that where there's a will, there's a way. Let us unveil our hidden strengths when invoking them in do-or-die situations. If you are going through rough times, please trust the internal voice telling you that you will overcome it and repeat aloud, "I can, I will, I have this."

This chapter will introduce my ghosts of deception, lies, cheating, betrayal and abandonment. In January 2017, Michael was close to completing the plans for Mercedes' university tours in Japan, Canada, North America and England. I found it strange being left out of all travel plans. He insisted I should not be selfish and let him and his daughter take the trips alone to bond before she went to university. I thought it was perhaps a bit late for bonding, but besides saying no, what else could I without sounding intrusive or mean.

To my surprise, Michael also made flight arrangements for my upcoming business trip. I usually took two weeks for quality inspection and meeting producers in various regions of Guatemala. I was baffled when Michael revealed my trip had turned into a two-month journey, claiming he had lost his job and needed to save money. Approaching were Chinese New Year and Easter celebrations. In the interest of saving money, Michael insisted,

"It's best if you avoid high season."

Feeling obliged to help somehow reduce family expenses, I reluctantly accepted. During Michael's and Mercedes' trip to London, they stayed at a hotel close to Portland Place in Marylebone. A day before my trip to Latin America, Mercedes showed up in Hong Kong. I was shocked; Michael unilaterally decided to send Mercedes alone on a 12-hour flight. When I asked about the "spontaneous" and rare decision, he suddenly claimed to get a lead for a job interview leaving him no choice but to remain in London. At the same time, Michael communicated switching from the hotel to a non-specified Airbnb to save money. I asked about the interview and his thoughts about moving back to London while our daughter had not finished high school. He resorted to his typical aggressive behavior. I stopped asking; I knew one of his nasty fits would come next. So, I instead wished him good luck with the interview.

Typical Michael, when he encounters an obstacle or problem he cannot solve, he resources to nasty tantrums and offensive behavior. During his burst of anger, he remembers everything and everyone he detests. It's a scary show. His mother was familiar with Michael's outbursts; his three sisters stopped talking to him for a long time because they could not stand his temper. The children and I trembled when we faced the episodes.

The list of people Michael detested included his previous employers in New York and Hong Kong. Apparently, Michael's tantrums were not welcome in Hong Kong, he wanted to simultaneously take command of different departments within the company. Still, he was drowning in all the work and responsibility. I think pride kept him from accepting that he couldn't handle the job. Michael began a campaign to make friends and enemies at work, and not soon after, he got dismissed. He is vengeful, and to take vengeance, he stole a unique and private financial trade, only known to one person in the company, his boss.

After speaking with one of his friends in New York, he proudly confessed, trying to sell it.

"I understand," Michael said, "I don't care if no money is made, perhaps only manipulate it to cause losses?"

When the call ended, I asked, "What trade?"
When I learned the details, I couldn't believe the insanity of holding such power to cause significant hurt. I reminded Michael that Symmetry had been good to us. I pointed out that he was out of work because of his

wrongdoings. But he was bitter about getting discharged and thought that holding the trade was the damage he could do to get them back.

Meanwhile, in Guatemala, I felt highly stressed and in a gloomy mood rather than the anticipated joy I expected when meeting new coffee growers. In a phone call, I asked Michael when he was planning to return to Hong Kong.

"If it's our daughter you worry about, she is in good hands with the helper" was his reply.

My trip in Guatemala got packed with visiting remote places in the highlands, coffee tastings, sampling, quality control inspections, learning more about organic grains, global warming on crops, visiting my suppliers, meeting new ones and understanding their needs. My days were busy, but once alone in a tiny hotel room in the Cuchumatanes Mountains, in the North-West of the country, sadness invaded my chest, and gloominess returned.

On 16 April 2017, Easter celebrations began; Holy Week in Guatemala is highly venerated. I was alone and far away from all of my family. During celebrations, businesses stopped operating, families got together, and most chose to head to the beaches in the Caribbean or the Pacific Ocean. Everybody working with me said goodbye and disappeared with grand plans.

My family had already made all their plans, some traveling abroad. I called Michael; it was around when he took our daughter to university touring in the US and Canada. I was again shocked to learn he decided to send her alone on a 17-hour flight back to Hong Kong.

Attempting to get more information about his reasons, I asked, "do you have another interview?"

Michael claimed the meeting proposal had also taken him by surprise. "I cannot tell you more, Diana; I don't want to jinx the outcome; so please stop asking; besides, I am already in New York."

"It's Easter, Michael. Should we get together? We are not far from each other; don't you feel alone? Is it OK if I fly to meet you?"

He reluctantly opposed. "Didn't I just tell you that I stayed behind for business? I need to prepare and read about the company. I have no time for fun. Please don't give me a hard time, do your work and let me do mine."

Without more to add, I claimed to understand. I certainly didn't want to trigger a fight. I asked Michael if I could make a two-hour flight and see our friend Patty in Sarasota, Florida.

"Fine," he replied, "look for an inexpensive ticket."

I wanted to see my friend Patty and spend a few days with her. She had become widowed not long ago. Her brother was also visiting. We teamed up to provide her with support and much-needed love.

As weeks passed, whenever I communicated with Michael, he seemed more aggressive, rude, and increasingly used derogative terms over the phone. I began dreading calling him unless it was necessary. When I returned to my town, I needed information about the surveying system on the property in Antigua that Michael had insisted on having. One camera was faulty. He was overcontrolling and required to know most of our doings or what took place on the property. It was sometimes impossible not to ask him about details. During my phone call with Michael, he was spewing profanities, calling me an idiot and useless for the simplest questions I asked. Alone, during evening hours, my head went around and around trying to figure out why Michael would go so out of his way to be so mean. I knew he was drinking more than usual, perhaps he was now abusing alcohol.

One morning, I was doing errands in Antigua. Knowing how much Michael liked collecting different riding jerseys, I stopped by a bicycle shop, took pictures of the available ones and offered to buy them for him.

"My love, do you like any of these? Give me a call." While waiting for his reply, a phone call came in. The call was to go to our 212-area code number in New York. The call would roll over to my phone when Michael didn't pick up. It was someone asking for him. I assumed it was an employer regarding his interviews in New York. To sound professional, I said that I was Michael's assistant and to leave a message. I took the phone number while standing in the bike shop. To ensure passing the correct information; I googled the company.

My legs weakened when I learned the caller was from a divorce law firm in New York. I called Michael instead of texting, got his voicemail and requested a callback.

When he finally called, I asked, "Is everything OK? Is there anything that I should know?

"Why?" he asked.

I told him about the phone call and passed on the message.

He called me crazy and began arguing about something else to divert my attention from the issue. To change the subject, I asked if he liked any of the jerseys from the pictures. He said no and asked me not to call him anymore and communicate only by text.

Finally, my business trip ended. I was excited to go back home. I left Guatemala on the afternoon on 4 May 2017 and arrived in Hong Kong the next day. Michael was like a fish out of water in public events. We had promised a friend leading an NGO named HOPE International with an event called "Clean Water For All"[10] to attend his fundraising event on 6 May. Michael needed me back in Hong Kong before the event to accompany him. It was a great opportunity for him to show his participation with the charity. I was fortunate to quickly find business connections for Michael wherever we went, including a few characters I wish would have never met or presented to my ex-husband.

My plane arrived 45 minutes late, Michael insisted on waiting for me at the airport. I saw him when I exited customs; he didn't smile. When I hugged him, he seemed distant and sour. I noticed a bit of nervousness in his behavior. He told me that he was worried for our daughter because she was waiting to have dinner with us; she was tired and had a test the next day. I thought it was bizarre to wait for me to dine with so much on her plate. I insisted on not being hungry and for us to dine at home. But Michael pressed we drop off my luggage at the front desk, collect our daughter and continue in the taxi to Stanley by the beach, about a 35-minute drive.

I also felt Mercedes was acting strange; she didn't want to hug me. I expressed how happy I was to see her. I also asked her if she didn't want to have dinner in Stanley; that was fine. Mercedes told me that she was happy to go. I expressed missing her a great deal and being in my prayers.

Mercedes turned abruptly and replied, "I don't want to hear about your religion. You're not a perfect example of it. I don't believe in God!"

Her comments left me utterly shocked. I reminded her of her 15th birthday, the beautiful church ceremony, her first communion and her guardian angels.

"I never wanted a party celebration. You did it because you wanted to party" she replied.

That hurt me. The effort and time I dedicated to make her feel special was all trash in a second. I was only gone for a short time, and now that I was back, my home and family were a madhouse with characters I could not recognize. Stupidly, I tried to explain to my daughter the supreme power, the goodness of spiritualism, and the power of belief. It's not religion; it's the power of faith. When you're alone, when everybody abandons you, and no one seems to care, faith gives you the strength to know that you are not alone. At that point, Michael jumped into the conversation and took her side.

"Let the child be, she is entitled to become an atheist if she wishes to do so."

I was dismayed and asked Michael to stop.

"We raised our children with spiritual beliefs, not necessarily Christian, so I think our daughter needs to analyze her reasoning. If she wishes to continue a path as an atheist, then so be it; but not tonight, not right now."

We arrived to Stanley, Mercedes chose the restaurant. Dinner continued with more tense conversations; it was agony being there. I couldn't wait for us to finish and go home.

At the end of the meal, we grabbed a taxi and headed home in silence. When we arrived, the apartment felt strange; something heavy floated in the air. Mercedes went to her room without saying goodnight. Michael went to the guest room. I stayed in the main bedroom, crying most of the night. The following day, the atmosphere in the house felt weird. The day went slow. I was jetlagged and confused about what had taken place the night before. Mercedes came from school and took a nap before the evening event. Michael and I hardly spoke during the day. We began to get ready for the gala night and coincided in the main bathroom; two-thirds of the walls were windows from floor to ceiling with views from the 59th floor gazing the green mountains of Mid-Levels East. So much beauty around us, yet I felt insipid during that time.

With disdain, Michael looked at me and said, "You look like your mother." As if my mother, who had been so kind to him, was a horrid creature.

A bit offended, I replied, "Well, of course Michael, I look like my mother; I'm her daughter!"

CHAPTER 6: SHOULD I STAY?

He changed the subject and replied, "You are taking too long."

I often thought that it was Michael, the one going mad. At that moment, that thought came back. Before going to the event, Michael held my hand and told me how beautiful I looked. We began with a pleasant feeling during dinner and managed to make some jokes and feel gay. There were raffles, competitions and dances. Our daughter looked pretty in a burgundy dress. She had a gorgeous smile on her face, and her big brown eyes had a spark of happiness. It was the first time since I returned from my trip that Mercedes and I were getting along well. We were laughing and participating in some of the games at the event. Michael also stopped being cruel and rude to me for a short time. At the end of the party, we were all invited to dance to the last piece. Several couples were already on the dance floor and I asked Michael to dance with me.

He replied, "Are you stupid? How do you think I will dance if no one else is dancing? No, I don't want to dance."

I looked at our daughter; she looked the other way avoiding eye contact. Finally, I said, "I will wait for you outside."

I waited about 15 minutes, then decided to take a taxi home. I had the impression Michael was waiting for me to leave before heading to the taxi stand. Not long later, Michael and Mercedes arrived.

He came to the main bedroom and began a fight with me; insulting me, and calling me crazy, and claiming I'd embarrassed him in front of our friends. Finally, I managed to stop him and clarified that I had already said my goodbyes, and no one noticed I was upset. But he was only interested in fighting. He grabbed his pillow and headed to the guest bedroom again.

That night, I must have slept one hour. The air was heavy; I felt the ceiling collapsing over me. A high-pitched noise kept ringing in my ears, making me nauseous. My luggage was on the corner, not yet unpacked. I called a friend named Debra; I needed to speak with someone. I cried like a baby over the phone, and I told her something was seriously wrong at home. In my desperation, I asked, "Please, tell me what to do."

Debra asked me a couple of questions and urged me to collect her keys from her concierge and stay at her place. Her home would be empty for three weeks until she returned to Hong Kong from Italy.

I got a flashback, and suddenly, my body trembled with fear. Before travelling to Guatemala, Michael said he had misplaced his house keys.

"Leave your set with me" he said. "After all, Mercedes and I will return before you after the university tours."

So, I left my set behind without hesitation, and now, I had no keys to my own home.

The next day I left the house to run a couple of errands. When I returned, the door was closed and locked. I considered the incident quite strange; there were two towers in the building, but each had its elevator. There was also one apartment per floor, and elevator keys only opened on the designated one, so we always kept our front door wide open. It took a while for Michael to respond to

CHAPTER 6: SHOULD I STAY?

my knocking. The helper was in the mezzanine; I asked her why the door closed and she went to her room without replying. I asked Michael why he locked the door.

"To make sure no undesirables get in" he replied.

I felt small and humiliated, but it did not stop me from standing up to him. I asked for my keys.

"What keys?" he replied.

Our poor daughter was already back from school and had to listen to the argument. As soon as I saw her, I asked for her keys.

"Yes, Mom" she said.

"NO!" Michael screamed from the kitchen.

"That key is yours Mercedes, don't give it to her."

"Not a big deal" she said, but Michael did not let her.

I grabbed the bags I had set aside, called an Uber, and left for Debra's house on the West side of Hong Kong Island.

The first night I spent at Debra's, I called Yunani, a dear friend from Indonesia. She heard the desperation in my voice. Yunani lived far away on Discovery Bay Island and had to take a ferry and taxi to meet me, but in less than an hour was at my door. When she saw me, she opened her arms, hugged me tight, and expressed concern for my wellbeing. She wiped my tears and sat with me through the night as we talked about many things to entertain my mind.

The following day, Yunani went back to her family. She called many times; and kept a watchful eye over my progress. I remember crying a lot, feeling confused and unable to join the dots of what was taking place. On the third day, I asked Michael to meet me; he selected a public café. Once we were face to face, he asked what I wanted. I replied, explanations and also money to travel. I needed to speak with my family in person and ask for their advice. I couldn't understand what was wrong, and asked for clues, but he was not giving me any. He turned things around and told me that it was me, the one constantly fighting with our daughter and making their life difficult. The coffee shop was loud, and we were surrounded by people. It made no sense to start getting into details. Michael was not paying attention; he was acting like a machine repeating absurdities over and over. I don't even remember what else was said. The meeting was short and unproductive. I left feeling emptier than when I arrived.

A message from my son David came through via the Signal App. He was asking how things were; I asked him to call me. When we spoke, I revealed things were not right. David in exchange told me something that surprised me a great deal. He said Mercedes had mentioned her father attending sessions with a psychologist in Hong Kong. She found out in February after the London trip. Michael had told our daughter I was crazy, that he couldn't deal with me any longer, and I was the reason for him seeking a psychologist's help. Mercedes must have also felt confused as she asked her father,

"I need to see a psychologist too. Can I also go?"

Michael was reluctant to grant her request. "I am not going any longer; the sessions are over" he replied.

It was not until much later that I understood why Mercedes wanted to see a psychologist. Michael managed to spend time alone with our daughter during the university tours; the rubbish he fed our daughter left her extremely confused and with poison in her heart. I asked David if he could arrange for his sister to call me. Mercedes and I communicated and decided to meet for coffee; I needed to talk to her in person. She suggested putting the invitation in the family chat so Michael could see it. From the beginning, I noticed how keen he was not to allow Mercedes spend time alone with me. As I suspected, Michael showed up at the coffee shop where Mercedes and I had agreed. As soon as he arrived, he was rude and insisted on knowing the specifics of the meeting. I replied that I needed to find out the source of the problem at home because I felt confused. I asked my daughter to tell me about the things that bothered her the most, and if there was anything I could change or do to help better our disagreements.

She told me that she wanted to be taken into consideration and that she wanted to be counted in family discussions and decisions. She was sixteen years old and would very soon be seventeen, many responsibilities were on her shoulders, but she also wanted her voice heard at home. So, I apologized to my daughter for sometimes taking her for granted.

I was talking when suddenly, Michael interrupted by saying that I didn't fit in the family, and it would be better if I didn't go back home. I stopped him sharp and once again directed my attention towards Mercedes. I asked her if she needed her mother—if she needed me back? I wanted her to choose what was best for her.

Mercedes said "Yes!"

In an aggressive manner, Michael interrupted again and ordered Mercedes to, "Go back home and do your homework"

She grabbed her schoolbag and left after Michael's command. Michael stayed behind. He told me with an angry tone that I should not go back.

"Why would you go back to a place where nobody wants you? I don't want you there" he said.

I replied, almost choking, "My daughter wants and needs me back; I am going back for her, not for you, Michael. If you don't like the idea, the one leaving should be you."

He slammed his hand on the table and left. After breathing and wiping tears, I left the coffee shop and headed to the taxi stand.

Before taking a taxi, I checked if Mercedes had arrived home. She was crying when she spoke.

"I am still on Mid-Level Mommy; I haven't left. Tell me where you are" she said, "I want to see you again."

Mercedes was around the corner; we met, hugged and cried on the street while pedestrians passing looked on in a judgmental manner for us not keeping face.

Finally, she said to me, "I don't understand what's wrong, I don't get it, but I know something is terribly wrong."

"Don't worry, baby" I said; "I'll go back today. I love you very much."

We walked together to the taxi stand. She nervously looked around, worrying her father would see us together.

CHAPTER 6: SHOULD I STAY?

"Why sweetheart" I said, "Why worry about your dad in that manner?"

She did not reply. The mental games Michael and his mistress used in a young, and vulnerable girl, is something to get tested in court for the damage they have caused.

I called Yunani and explained what took place. To my luck, she was off from work; she took the next ferry and met me in Kennedy Town at Debra's place. Yunani wanted to make sure Michael would not see me alone; she helped me grab my belongings and we headed to my place. Our apartment was on the 59th floor. The front door of our flat was closed. I still didn't have my key. We rang the doorbell several times. Finally, Michael came over and opened. Not realizing my friend was behind, he asked what I wanted there. Yunani and I made our way inside. Mercedes was having dinner; we passed by the kitchen and said hello to her, then went upstairs to the main bedroom and dropped off my bags. Yunani asked me if I had dinner, and I replied negatively. So, we agreed to eat before she went back home.

We passed the kitchen again; Michael was now sitting next to Mercedes.

"Mommy, did you eat?"

"No, I haven't, sweetheart. I will go with Yunani and then be right back."

Michael ignored us and continued with his back to the kitchen door.

After saying goodbye to Yunani at the ferry terminal, I returned home. The atmosphere was oppressive. I felt as if there was no oxygen. The 20-foot-high ceiling felt like it was collapsing in on my head. Michael was with Mercedes in her room. I said goodnight to Mercedes and went to the main bedroom, took a shower, put on my pajamas and tried to get some sleep in vain.

From that day on and for the next several months, I would sleep one, two, maybe three hours a night, and sometimes wouldn't sleep at all. I began to lose my appetite; all food tasted like cardboard. When my daughter was around, Michael would try to pick fights with me, so she would see me upset. When he was with our daughter, he pretended I was not there. When Mercedes was at school, he would pass next to me and spew vile comments.

The mental abuse was incessant. Anxiety attacks controlled my days; my eyes became incredibly irritated and dry from crying. I had to visit an eye specialist and get medicine to stop my corneas from getting damaged. My only happy distractions were waiting for coffee shipments and contacting coffee connoisseurs in Hong Kong. My goal was to get well-known baristas to train and compete the following year with my coffee, pride of my faraway land.

My appearance was horrible; I was very thin, the fast weight loss made me look sickly and the lack of appetite continued. I wanted to attend church services but didn't want to return to the usual venue; I wasn't ready for comments and questions. Then, an acquaintance told me about a non-denominational Christian church close to home. She mentioned the church had a strong community and a with many families attending. So, I gave it a try. It was a beautiful experience that made me feel at peace for the first time in weeks.

At the beginning of May 2017, I felt as if home and our family had been shipped to hell. Everything happened so quickly. Mercedes was working on a final art piece for the year-end exhibition. She knew I had an eye for art, and many times she asked me about colors, content and my opinion about the pieces she was working on. We agreed to work together on a piece; we wanted to show what the two of us were going through at the time. It was her idea; I got to model for the artist. The final details included a constellation in the background, adding a terrific effect to the piece of art.

Laying on the ground, I was dressed in a simple ankle-length white dress, three leaves over my pubic bone and barefoot. My curly hair formed an aura accompanied by red roses intertwined with green ivy. I felt as if sent into the Milky Way, ignorant, naked, powerless and questioning how to help my daughter if I could hardly help myself?

In less than three months, my husband turned into a greater monster, dragging our daughter with deception into unimaginably low tactics to cause chaos and hurt. At the time, I still could not figure out what was going on; feeling trapped in a nightmare, I finally asked Michael if he would agree to see a family therapist. I'm not sure the extent of the lies Michael fed our daughter, calling them, accordingly to Mercedes, their little "secrets". However, he reluctantly agreed when I confronted him by asking about the therapy he had when I was away. Michael attempted to dismiss me by claiming he needed to talk to someone after getting discharged from his job in August 2016 and founding himself in a crossroads situation.

His words made no sense to me; Michael had opted to take life insurance policy benefiting himself with a yearly premium of $187,100 USD and take a year off to relax before looking for his next job. So, nothing told me he was financially worried. Of course, I knew little about our total savings, but if he was so relaxed about the situation, I trusted we were economically secure. The business card of the psychologist Michael had seen was among piles of his paper on a desk of our home office. Before speaking with Michael about family therapy, I called and asked if the practice accepted families and couples for treatment. The receptionist checked the doctor's name and confirmed with a yes. After asked a couple of questions, I got offered optional appointment dates. So, my first instinct was to visit the same place to make things easier and cost-effective. When I proposed my idea to Michael, I could see how shocked he was about my findings but didn't back down. Check with them if you want, he said. It wasn't even ten minutes since Michael and I had spoken when I called for an appointment. This time the reply was negative, the receptionist confirmed that Dr. Lori Chau (of Central Minds, Hong Kong), was no longer accepting new patients.

Glancing at the practice web page, I found that Dr. Chau had a partner who, unlike her, held a PhD and was well-praised by clients. Unfortunately, several phone calls later, it turned out she wasn't working at the practice any longer. So, a little more googling led me to a big surprise

CHAPTER 6: SHOULD I STAY?

when I found out that the PhD psychologist was also a minister for a non-denominational Christian church.

I was excited to tell Michael about my findings. He was pretty surprised I had sourced somebody in such a short time. I called the practice and stated that the appointment was urgent. The psychologist said she did not have any space at her usual practice but could see us at a clinic where she performed community service for a church. When I learned the address, to my surprise, it was the same church I had visited just one week ago.

The meeting with Dr. Michele Bland turned out to be an actual circus. Michael appeared to be well-coached on what to say. He asked to speak first and was allowed to do so. Michele provided ground rules; no interrupting was one of them. While Michael spoke, the lies began pouring out of his mouth like Niagara Falls. I was biting my tongue and pinching my hands to the point of bleeding. I could not stop crying when Michael said he was afraid because I was crazy, dangerous and fearful for his life.

When I was allowed to speak, Michael interrupted me over and over. I felt intimidated by how he looked at me and decided to ask Michele for help, "Dr. Bland, please ask him to adhere to the rules so I can speak."

I saw the expression of concern on Michele's face. But despite being an expert in her field, she seemed lost on how to control Michael's aggressive behavior. Neither Dr. Bland nor I were ready for the mess unveiled in that meeting. He told the psychologist that it was a huge mistake to marry me and that our family's problem was me. Michael insisted that I was planning to take our daughter away from him and was worried about her well-being. I glanced at Michele and asked her to steer the conversation into something constructive.

I even asked Michael if he wanted the divorce, "Why not say so instead of going through a painful show?"

Finally, I got to the point of despair and could not take it any longer. I knew how Michael operates and there was very little that would make him stop. I asked to get excused, and I left the consultation room in tears. Days after we met with Dr. Bland, I found out that Michael was not looking for a solution to "our" problems but instead hoping to get a witness to his already big plan. To Michael's frustration, his tactic did not work, as I walked away with dignity that day, and he did not get the pleasure of him making me look crazy.

Sunday came and I went to church. The service splits into two different sections across two separate buildings; on one side, families and small children, in the other room primarily the elderly and adults. I went to the family section. When the church service was over, I saw Michelle and the other Minister saying goodbye to both groups. She saw me and suggested that I give her a call the next day. Michelle wanted to try for our family, or at least Michael and me, to attend church together. I proposed reluctantly, and Michael accepted. So next Sunday, only Michael and I went to the service. He brought his bicycle and cycling clothes. His plan was to cycle Lantau Island and visit our friends; neither Mercedes nor I got invited to go with him. At the end of the service, all those needing special prayers got invited to stay behind and go to the front.

CHAPTER 6: SHOULD I STAY?

I asked Michael, shall we go? He said yes, so we went and asked for prayers. Everything seemed normal until the lady offering the prayers asked us to express the intent of our prayers. I requested prayers for our marriage, our children, my husband and peace. Michael became enraged and began arguing.

"So, it is always about you," he said. "Why isn't anyone asking me what I want?"

He walked away, leaving the lady offering the prayers and me perplexed by his behavior.

I caught up with Michael in the front garden before he took off on his bicycle. I grabbed his arm and asked, "What in hell was wrong with you?"

Dr. Bland approached us and asked Michael what was wrong. He said he was very upset because nobody ever asked what he wanted.

"Today I wanted to have a pleasant Sunday, take a ferry, ride my bike and visit our friends, but Diana ruined my Sunday!"

I felt embarrassed for Michelle to witness Michael's typical tantrums. I thanked Minister Michelle Bland and walked away, trying to find a taxi as soon as possible. An awful feeling of loneliness invaded me with a mix of pain and confusion, too complex to put into words. Michael returned home very late, drunk and without saying a word went to sleep in the guest bedroom. I was so confused that I blamed myself for ruining Sunday for the whole family. Slowly but constantly, I recalled incidents that should have triggered alarm bells, such as the matter of our wills.

A Will?

It was always a great concern that Michael and I travel often, and most of the time together. I insisted on him setting up our final wishes in a legal document; it was essential to leave the children protected in case of an accident. Towards the end of 2016, Michael finally produced some papers from a company in the US doing financial planning. However, the whole thing was a lie. Michael deceived me by pretending he was working on our wills. Instead, he was working on his life insurance worth $3 million USD, for him to receive at the age of 65. After losing his job in August of 2016, Michael was drinking heavily. He said to be drinking more than usual because he felt stressed but decided that he would take one year off to relax despite "feeling" stressed.

I inquired about our wills and the papers I found about his decision to take such expensive premium life insurance. He was good with words. He knew how to convince people and knew exactly what, how and when to say it. He stated his decision benefited the family and helped keep our money safe; we could borrow money against it, pay ourselves interest, and not pay any taxes or penalties. Michael also insisted that the life insurance would take care of the children and myself if something happened to him. Finally, he pointed out the area where I was his designated successor, and for me not to worry about the "will" as everything was being taken care of.

Michael often asked me to sign documents. I never asked any questions because I knew he would get aggressive and throw a tantrum if I got too much into the details. He insisted on managing our money and investments and also handled all of the bank accounts. So, I was only needed when there was time to sign whatever he wanted me to sign. During our marriage, we had bank accounts in the US, England, Hong Kong, Canada, and Jersey. All bank accounts were under both of our names. Little did I know that in reality I didn't have access to most of them. Michael was the primary account holder, and he could change everything with a simple click or phone call.

He never shared the bank security keys or passwords to our global banking under false pretexts of having a complex banking system. Instead, he claimed it was best if only he would manage the online banking. He asked me to generate spreadsheets to count out-of-country data for tax records and bank interest gained. Only because of the spreadsheets did I become aware of the bank balances. But I was restricted from accessing them. Even when I had to make bank transfers, I had to request Michael to do it for me. I got trained to depend on him, and it was scary to realize how much power he had over me.

The atmosphere at home was horribly tense. While running errands one day, I called Mercedes and asked if she wanted to have dinner. She got excited about the idea, and we set a time and place to dine. A few minutes later, I received a call from Michael. He was furious and exhorted that he and our daughter had agreed to have dinner together, same day every week. He accused me of intentionally attempting to spoil things for them. I had no clue that such an arrangement existed, and his screams left me trembling while waiting for transport to take me back home. Attempting to calm Michael's anger, I called back and invited him to join the dinner, but he refused. I also asked Mercedes to invite her father, but instead, he threw one of his typical tantrums and refused Mercedes too. Although I also thought about inviting Michael in person, when I got home, Michael had already left. My daughter and I took a taxi and headed to the restaurant. We had a good time; laughed and talked endlessly about all sort of things.

When we returned home, Mercedes needed tape and asked me to get it from the office. I turned on the lights, and Michael's briefcase was wide open. Several bank cashier's checks were made to Michael's name, and withdrawing slips, checks for $776,697 Hong Kong Dollars (HKD), $170,000 US Dollars (USD), £30,000 Great British Pounds (GBP) and further $30,000 Hong Kong Dollars. In addition, a yellow receipt from divorce solicitors from a consultation performed 10 May 2017. My heart stopped, and I ran back to Mercedes' bedroom with a document in hand.

"Do you know what these are?"

"No." she replied.

"This is money from our joint accounts; your father withdrew it and transferred it to his name."

I begged her not to say anything about it and that I would hide them. Then, when Michael asks, I would discuss with him. I hide the cashier's checks behind one of Mercedes' paintings in the living room.

CHAPTER 6: SHOULD I STAY?

Michael came home very late and highly intoxicated; without acknowledging me, went to the bathroom, brushed his teeth, grabbed his pajamas, and headed to the guest bedroom. Something told me to switch the checks to another location.

The following morning, Mercedes was having breakfast; I heard Michael screaming and summoning me. He was questioning our daughter in the kitchen. He wanted to know who had taken the checks. Mercedes was very upset with her father, but fear of him overcame her. I saw my daughter trembling and pointing out where she saw me hiding them. Michael rushed to the painting, but I had followed my instinct and moved them to another place. Enraged and with a look of an unstable person, Michael grabbed me by the shoulders, shook me and demanded me to hand over the checks; without faltering, I denied having them. Michael picked up the handset to call the concierge for a taxi and headed to the elevator, but not without cursing at me first. I had the feeling he was running to HSBC's head office in Central; I got ready and did the same.

I knew the bank's Premier Centre was on the fourth floor; attempting not to cross paths with Michael, I headed to the third floor and requested to speak with the manager. Despite shaking and feeling scared, I spoke clearly and directly. I knew that it was my only opportunity to get my point across, and I had to do it right. Explaining the problem, I emphasized that all bank accounts were joint. How was it possible for my husband to withdraw all of our money without my consent? I saw the manager literally running back and forth, trying to get information. She was mystified about how Michael was able to achieve the transactions. The building has a glass atrium in which all floors open up to the center of the building. I could hear Michael screaming at the Premier Representative on the fourth floor,

"You have to replace my cashier's checks!"—his usual way to intimidate and confuse people was at play.

The manager on the third floor asked me to get on the phone because the Premier Manager had a couple of questions for me. First, she asked me to confirm if the checks had gone missing.

To that I replied, "No, I actually have them right here with me."

Then I was asked to speak to Michael over the speaker. Mrs. Hieb, please tell your husband where the checks are. So, I did.

"You know what you are saying is untrue, Michael; the checks are not lost, you know I have them. Premier Manager, please do not replace them; I said you do not have my consent."

Just imagine Michael not being in control. It was a blow to his ego, so he acted accordingly by screaming and demanding I get off the phone, but I had already made my point, and no check replacement would be taking place. Michael was furious; I heard him cursing at everyone in his path. After he left the bank, I went to the Premier Center. I agreed with both managers to make an official joint deposit. Michael and I would redeposit the checks in the presence of one of them.

CHAPTER 6: SHOULD I STAY?

Looking back, I should have protected the family money better; it was not clever what I did. Unfortunately, my lack of knowledge and integrity did not allow me to think of any other alternative. So, the children and I paid the price. I'm unsure how many days went by before Michael emptied our bank accounts again. He transferred our money to a company he recently founded in Hong Kong and other bank accounts, including two new sole accounts in England and New York.

The morning after I found the checks; I called my mother-in-law in Colorado, USA. I was in distress. At the time, I used to call Sharon "Mom." I asked her if she knew anything about Michael's behavior and the issue with the money. I mentioned that many strange things were taking place at home and asked if she had a clue about it. What Sharon revealed left me cold and more confused. She told me that Michael called her a few days before I arrived from my business trip in Guatemala. He confessed to her contacting every prominent solicitor in Hong Kong, so they could not speak with me if I were to get in touch. Sharon is a good music and substance abuse therapist, but unfortunately strange to her children. It was odd that Michael would call to confide in her with such a bizarre revelation. Was he again getting coached? A few days after the incident with the bank, I asked Michael for money to consult a solicitor. Instead, I received a promise that he would write a check to the legal entity willing to see me. Unfortunately, Sharon was absolutely correct; none of the high-profile divorce solicitors wanted to speak with me.

I called my friend Regina, a non-practicing lawyer living in Hong Kong. She helped me with a referral to a solicitor who finally agreed to see me. Carolyn McNally turned out to be a fantastic solicitor. We met and went over several of my concerns. I also made her aware about the issue with the money and physical and mental abuse. In the meantime, Michael ended up with our money at his disposal, leaving me at his mercy and able to track my moves.

Michael's mysterious phone calls were becoming more frequent, and he bolder about receiving them. If I was around, he usually grabbed the phone and headed to the garden area, 59 floors below. Observing her father's behavior, Mercedes recounted having lunch with Michael. He received a phone call; he never had a problem speaking about business, friends or relatives when we were around. This time, she felt curious about the call, went around the table and approached Michael. Michael pushed her away, became very angry and left the table to answer the call. Mercedes was shaken and upset; she grabbed her bag and returned home alone.

When Michael got home, he scolded her, demanding never again to get close when answering a call. It was scary being around his erratic behavior. Mercedes and I noticed Michael excessively drinking. It was unsettling finding his bottles of vodka in the office, bathroom, closet, and other weird places like shoe racks. He stopped caring if Mercedes and I were around and began locking himself in the office to answer mysterious calls. I knew that something was terribly wrong, but I remained disoriented.

CHAPTER 6: SHOULD I STAY?

By then, I weighed 43kg and was sleep-deprived, looking pale as a ghost and my eyes in terrible shape. Mercedes left to go to school and I needed to get out of the house. At the same time, I was weak and without much strength, whenever I could, I'll try to remember important events to help me find answers. My head kept gathering pieces of the puzzle, and a flashback came about Michael's sudden acquisitions. In December 2016, Michael invested a big chunk of our money in Gojoko, his British friend's company based in London. He was also thinking about investing in AMP Credit Technologies, owned by an American man named Stein. His wife Argely is from Colombia and was also a member of the Spanish Speaking Women's Association in Hong Kong. Stein was a mystery to many unless his wife would make an introduction.

She would take notice of husbands in banking and investments businesses. When Argely learned about Michael's background in finance, she was desperate to set up a meeting with her husband. I deeply regret that introduction. By January 2017, Michael had decided to invest $200,000 USD of our family money in Stein's company. I criticized the decision and reminded him of being unemployed. Michael replied that Stein was clever and helped ex-pats hide money and avoid taxes, especially if they are from the US. I asked what was smart about that.

Michael replied, "Well, many of those are here in Hong Kong." I disagreed, but Michael did not care; his plans were much worse than I could have imagined.

Around April 2017, Michael began inquiring about how and who helped me register my business. Finally, towards the end of May, he registered his consulting company named Balan Core Ltd., with an opening balance of $500,000 HKD. With the consent of his new best friend, Stein, Michael used AMP Credit Technology's address, paid one person working for AMP and declared paying salary for one of Bahlam Core Ltd.'s employees. He also ramped the capital to $1 Million HKD from the family money and pretended to be recruiting to make his company seem thriving.

The Divine Power Has My Back

Michael spent most of the time at AMP Credit Technologies, or so he said. He got up late, around 10 a.m., read the newspaper, followed by a leisurely breakfast, called for a taxi and headed to Stein's office, where he had a desk.

One day though, Michael left later than usual; I walked past the closed door of our home office. I overhead Michael speaking about the kidnapping. He sounded agitated, and did not seem to notice he was speaking loudly. The room had one wall made out of glass, allowing his voice to amplify even more. Michael said "she" was stupid and went further by speaking about getting her to disappear. I thought it must be some joke or reference to a book. I had enough issues bothering me, so I decided not to overthink the conversation. But following this conversation, for some reason I paid closer attention to Michael's closed doors conversations, mainly because they became more frequent and animated.

CHAPTER 6: SHOULD I STAY?

On 29 May 2017, I found myself pacing back and forth, feeling trapped and suffocating as if in a cage. I wished Michael a good day and left for a short walk. The weather was hot and muggy but I didn't care, I needed an escape. The night before, I had a terrible anxiety attack. In the middle of the night, I got on my knees. My heart racing, and my eyes hurting from crying. I asked God, the Divine Power, if he loved me. Why wasn't He helping me? I pleaded to please reveal the truth of what was going on and to give me guidance. You have given the promise for us to ask, and we should receive. I am now asking, tell me the truth.

I had left the building for my walk, and as I stepped onto the path, a soft but clear voice told me to return home. I looked—there was no one around. Am I going crazy, I murmured to myself. Then the voice again; in a more insisting tone, "Go back home…go, back, home." My heart began racing. I walked up the hill back to the building as fast as possible, grabbing the elevator to the 59th floor. The elevator door opened into the living room.

Every time the elevator would reach our floor, a loud ding, ding was heard all over the apartment. As if perfectly prepared to suit the occasion, the helper vacuuming the living room, allowed me to return without alerting Michael. I asked the helper for my husband's whereabouts. Irosha replied in the guest bedroom behind closed doors. We had a policy of no shoes in the house. So, there were no footsteps against the shiny caramel color parquet floors. Before knocking on the door, I noticed that it was not a business call.

I thought perhaps Michael was talking to his mother; the 12-hour difference made it evening time in the US. If he was talking to Mom, I would interrupt and say hello. Thinking that I was not around, Michael spoke somewhat agitatedly and loudly. He laughed and said that Diana was scared. When I heard that, I thought my heart would jump out of my chest. My heart was beating so fast, and my hands got sweaty. I suddenly had an urge to turn on my phone and began recording the conversation. My phone was about 10 inches away from me and close to the door. My palpitations were so intense I got afraid Michael could hear them from inside. I heard how the person talking with Michael guided him into the different steps he was to follow. How to make me look and sound insane, which procedures constituted insanity, and how to carefully record my moves. They talked about me being scared, how stupid I was, how useless our children were and how much they needed Mercedes and their need to keep her on their side. The conversation went on and on about getting rid of me.

I had no idea, no clue why. Michael began calling the woman on the other side "baby". He said to the woman not to worry, "I will find a job in the United States; I can make a very good living there. We don't need to worry about people criticizing us".

The two continued to discuss things about our children. My head was spinning, wondering who she was? Why does she know so much about the children and me? Why do they want to make me disappear? Why do they want to get me out of the way? I heard Michael laughing sarcastically, saying, "She is so horrible, even kidnapers will return her."

I was numb—suddenly, a voice with an insistent tone told me, "Enough!" I stopped recording and ran upstairs to the main bathroom; Michael almost caught me running up the stairs. I turned on the shower and began undressing.

Michael heard the water running, rushed to the bathroom and looked surprised to see me there.

"When did you get back?"

"Just now" I said.

"Weren't you supposed to go for a walk?"

"Unfortunately, it was too hot; I was not feeling well, so I returned."

He exited the bathroom, called for a taxi and left the apartment. I couldn't believe what I had just witnessed. Was Michael so evil that he was really attempting to get me killed? Despite my shock, all I could think was if God had really spoken to me. Deep inside, I believe He did.

For the rest of the day, I felt in limbo. My mind became a factory of awful thoughts. My body shook uncontrollably; I vomited everything I put in my mouth. Every step I took felt as if an electric current traveled from my shoulders to the bottom of my spine. I prayed, asking for guidance on what to do with the avalanche about to happen. My main concern was Mercedes, for her not to experience any more arguments, for me not to cause her more pain. Things were not right at home, but Michael was not going to clarify anything to our daughter, I was unsure of how I could explain to her that her father was using and manipulating her with such cowardly intents.

The following day, Mercedes had a tutoring session at 11 a.m. Once she was gone, I noticed Michael was playing with his computers in our home office. I asked him if I could speak with him and proceeded to close the door. With all the strength I had, I kept my composure and asked if it was anything I should know or anything that he needed to tell me. He looked at me as if I had three heads and said,

"No…if you're here to fight, I'm not in a mood."

"Michael, I love you, or I think I do. If you want the divorce, I will give it to you. We were not born together and probably will die at different times; we don't need to remain together unless we want to."

He immediately told me that I was crazy.

"I don't think so" I said.

"Please follow me to the bedroom as I have something important I wish you to hear".

By then, the recording of him and his mistress was already on my computer. He reluctantly followed me; I closed and locked the door. Then played the recording on the loudest mode. When Michael began hearing his voice and calling me stupid, his facial expression transitioned from a bully to a coward.

"What is that, sweetie?"

I reply, "It's you and another woman, so have the courtesy to tell who that person is. Why do you want to get rid of me?"

CHAPTER 6: SHOULD I STAY?

He got closer, and I began shaking, not knowing what he may do. He referred to the woman as an old friend of long ago, something stupid, perhaps a mid-life crisis. All happened over the phone, he said. I had no reason to believe him, so insisted pressing on to learn who the accomplice was, who would destroy a family? Who could be so mean? And you, coward, cannot even ask for a divorce? Michael is an expert bully and used his interrogating techniques on the children and me countless times. It was time to give him a bit of his own medicine. So, I insisted until he told me,

"It's Lina, your friend."

My world crumbled. I felt ashamed, upset, and even worried for Lina's husband and young child.

"Michael, she's married, why her? Poor Bryan."

And as if it was a conversation about what to have for dinner, his guilt disappeared.

"Sweetie, it was nothing serious; it really did not mean anything; Bryan knows about it."

"Oh, Michael" I said. "Something is terribly wrong; if it is true that Bryan knows, please pick up the phone and call him right now; I want to hear Bryan telling me so."

I noticed how nervous Michael became, "No, not right now, it's too early in Texas."

"OK, then I will call" I said.

"NO!" Michael begged. "Give me a few hours; right now, is not a good time; Bryan may be with Lina."

"What do you mean Bryan is with Lina?"

"Well, of course, he may be, Bryan is her husband!"

"Please, let's wait a few hours, just a few hours!", he pleaded.

Attempting not to cause more trouble, I accepted. In retrospect, I hate myself for doing so. I should have called Bryan and run to the police to report a kidnapping attempt which I had heard behind a closed door. But foolishly I trusted Michael to do the right thing, a lesson now learnt; a selfish, narcissistic, and abusive person doesn't easily change, especially not overnight.

Chapter 7

The Abuser

The man I once loved was slowly killing me. It was sad to observe Lina, a woman I once called friend, in a dysfunctional, manipulative and evil mode. She betrayed her husband and abandoned her young child and did not seem troubled by it. With quite a bit of experience, having been married three times before, she knew how to manipulate, especially with a psychology degree. Her background should have raised red flags, but it was hard to detect to those who don't cheat or are poisoned with envy.

To help control my nervous state, I talk to myself with positive affirmations, first quietly and then aloud, reaffirming I was strong and able to overcome. Insomnia became a partner every single night. Learning about grounding helped me a great deal. I began hugging trees, walking barefoot in the grass, touching leaves and flowers, and meditating in the park. I remember the days when all I wanted was to die. But I had too many good people around me who never let me forget my true value.

There is no such thing as a little bit of a lot of abuse. Abuse is abuse; and learning to identify it could save your life. It's tough to confront it, and it is never easy to admit we are victims to our family and friends. For me, it was essential to do so. In the beginning, nobody believed I was the victim. For years, I concealed Michael's true character and painted a picture of a man I wanted everyone to admire. Then, after I requested for divorce, Michael convinced many people that it was me, the unfaithful one, crazy and the source of our family problems. He is a toxic person, and when he could no longer control me, he tried to control how others saw me. He prostituted himself for a campaign to destroy my reputation and almost succeeded. But in the end, other people saw the truth, just like I had; it is about loyalty, something Michael knows nothing about.

We must remember that we are worth it, and there is nobody who will fix our life unless we get the courage to do it ourselves. We were born alone and will probably die alone. The rest is a choice. Sometimes I feel ashamed for the many things I tolerated. One thing is for sure, I have learned my lesson. Peace and happiness: it's the ultimate goal. I cannot change what happened. However, I can look forward to knowing that I, most certainly, would never make the same mistakes.

CHAPTER 7: THE ABUSER

Deception

Once I had confronted Michael, he confessed to what had happened in 2015, the night of our daughters' birthday. He said Lina needed to speak with him in private, preferably after everyone had gone to sleep. So, the pair met at around 2 a.m. and Michael brought drinks to our home office located on the mezzanine floor. According to Michael, Lina was crying, desperate and feeling suicidal. She was heading for another divorce. As per Michael, Lina and Bryan were having marital problems. She claimed Bryan was impotent. I found her statement strange, as it was the same excuse she had used in previous divorces.

Michael asked Lina why she didn't ask me for help. She cleverly replied, "Diana will judge me. Since you are also my friend, perhaps you can help more without making me feel guilty".

I could not believe what Michael was telling me. It became apparent she was a con artist, wanting pity and to entangle Michael in her lies. I asked him if he had looked for an opportunity to speak with Bryan?

"No...Lina did not allow it" he replied.

"What do you mean allowed?"

Apparently, she had worked an intricate plan to play Michael and her husband simultaneously to the expenses of my "fake madness".

In 2016, looking into secure messenger services, Michael told me that WhatsApp and Skype were not trustworthy and kept Skype only to communicate with his mother in Colorado. I recall asking him why he had such a careful need to guard in a messaging app.

"It's not like you work for the secret service."

"You never know..." he replied.

In May 2017, I still had no idea of the mess Michael had created by getting involved with Lina. I only knew of the "phone call" I overheard. I remember Michael buying a new phone and pairing it with his old one; he ran an errand leaving one charging in the office. I looked at the phone, and the idea that all the answers I needed were in Michael's phone overcame me. The advanced technology and his knowledge of computer programming intimidated me. He often shared his phone password with Mercedes and me to set hotspots or listen to music. What if he changed his access? What if he realized I was messing with the phone? I got scared and was about to walk away, but I decided to tap on his phone screen. Suddenly, the phone opened. No password was needed. While pairing his phones, Michael had left the phone unlocked.

I learned that he used Signal to keep his conversations with his mistress. Lina had a long list of calls registered in his "secure" phone. In addition, she had begun with the controlling techniques by asking Michael to send pictures of his daily routine. He was also to call her at specified times. I remember Lina telling me, her family and friends that studying psychology would not feed her daughter. Still, it would undoubtedly help her understand herself, or was it to learn how to better manipulate? If the efforts, and amount of thinking, criminals used to plan their crimes were put into benefiting society, this world would be a better place.

Michael was already a paranoid person and became obsessed with security during his affair with Lina. He kept IP addresses and servers in Singapore, the USA, England, Guatemala, Hong Kong and Brazil. Michael was proud of his vast knowledge of Linux and several other computer languages and bragged about making his home server and computers impenetrable. I will let the authorities be the judge of that.

On Michael's phone, I found their secret travel plans for Michael and his mistress, how to manipulate my daughter Mercedes and use the trips to visit universities to see each other. In addition, there were travel plans for Lina to meet Michael, hotel reservations and how to orchestrate sending Mercedes by herself from New York and London back to Hong Kong while I was on my business trip.

There were emails and documents about Lina asking Michael to pay her $80,000 USD student loan she had carried since college. The same college loan she was seeking to satisfy when she asked me to lend her money during our trip to Texas in 2016. I also found a record of Michael leaving the hotel he stayed with our daughter in London and when he moved to the Airbnb where he and Lina stayed after getting rid of her. Unlike hotels, Airbnb's have no cameras. So, I guess Michael felt safe that way. I also found thousands of pounds in alcohol purchases and rental car receipts to the English countryside. Bills of a cottage rental. Many other expenses, and not even one trace of a job interview. By then, I was not even hoping to find one.

Michael was responsible for setting up alternative email accounts and phone numbers for Lina. He also began changing his and her passwords. The duo had details of manipulating Mercedes, when and how they would use her, and how to keep the child on their side. They carefully studied what triggered my anxiety, what made me lose control, pushed me into depression and ultimately claiming my insanity. For once, Lina was doing a professional job.

At the end of the second university tour in New York and Canada, Michael flew to Dallas, Texas, and stayed in a hotel where he met Lina, and spent the night together. The following day, the pair drove to her family's home for Michael to say hello to Bryan. Lina's madness went beyond an unimaginable web of manipulation and lies.

Lina had told her husband that Michael had confirmed me being insane, and he needed help. She was our friend and, coincidently, a psychologist. Thus, deciding to help Michael and spend countless hours "counseling" him. Bringing Michael to her house would help her seal a load of her infamous lies fed to her husband. Lina began asking for details about me. She would compare her marriage troubles to mine and come up like a wife who knew how to handle the same problems, but better, to the point that Michael began asking her for advice.

In Colorado, USA, Christopher Watts is serving a life sentence for killing his pregnant wife and two young daughters for his mistress. I cannot stop thinking of how some people turn into dangerous monsters by doing unimaginable things for totally selfish reasons.

Stein and His Companies

I was at a loss with Michael's behavior. He didn't have many friends of his own. I became afraid of his mental health. I was also worried about mine, but I had a good set of friends. So, I decided to commit the big mistake of asking Stein to meet me. His wife, Argely, didn't know about my marital problems. So, I requested Stein to meet on a confidential basis. Stein was divorced, and I thought he could understand many things Michael and I couldn't.

"Stein you are spending a reasonable amount of time with Michael; he doesn't have many friends, perhaps you can help him."

Stein agreed; we met at Pacific Place in Causeway Bay. I told him how I had found out about the affair. I also knew Stein and Argely attended monthly Christian services led by a Colombian group trying to make their way in Hong Kong. So, I thought he would understand the surreal events I experienced. I told Stein that it was clear Michael wanted to divorce, so why not just make things easy by going ahead with the process instead of pretending. Was it that Michael's ego didn't allow him to accept a lost fight?

"Please talk to him. I think he needs help putting his thoughts in order, or Mercedes and I will continue to suffer a great deal."

Stein promised to help. I thanked him, and we said goodbye. The same night, Michael went out with Stein; he came home next day in the early hours. He was intoxicated, and before going to the guest bedroom, he woke me up.

"I had a great chat with Stein. He sends his regards. He told me that you had done a great job by telling him about what was happening at home. I want you to know that you sound ridiculous telling people stories about voices. I knew you were crazy; your meeting with Stein confirms you are insane. I now have a witness who is willing to corroborate."

I could not believe what I had just heard. But knowing Michael had turned into a liar, I sent a text to Stein.

"What is going on? You promised to help; did you make things worse?"

When Stein replied, he asked, "Why? You asked me to help Michael, precisely what I did."

Michael had invested a good amount of our money in Stein's company, and it became evident where his loyalty lay. A conversation Michael and I had in December 2016 came to mind.

"Diana, investing in AMP Credit Technology is the best I can do for now. Stein is clever; he told me how things inside AMP work."

After 12 years of being married to Argely, a Colombian woman he met in Hong Kong, Stein refused to give her US citizenship. Michael said it was beautifully set up. Apparently, Stein was the mastermind. He married Argely and made her a financial investor. She got her permanent

CHAPTER 7: THE ABUSER

Hong Kong residency, and then Stein put all his business in her name (of course, after she signs all rights back to him). Argely kept Colombian citizenship and pretended that Stein was only her employee, thus keeping the US worldwide tax authorities in the dark about the vast amount of money made. As a result, money was washed through Colombia, the Philippines, the UAE and several other countries.

I remember remarking how disgusting it was that a Colombian woman was used as a mule in a white-collar scheme. The worst was when I learned that the real aim of AMP Credit Technology was to help ex-pats, mainly from the US and the UK, avoid taxes and report income overseas. Further into my story, during court proceedings in London, I realized how dangerous it was to have two criminals pulling ropes to mislead my case.

It was almost impossible to hide from Mercedes how bad things were at that time. She continued to hear the heated arguments between Michael and me. Ultimately, she grew concerned about the real issue behind the troubles at home. She started listening behind doors and one day confronted us and asked for the truth; Michael denied any wrongdoing. In contrast, I told our daughter that Michael was having an affair with Lina. Michael insisted on no such an affair.

"I told you before that your mother is crazy," he replied.

Michael promised Mercedes that we would work things out. But then again, we had Dr. Jekyll and Hyde at home.

Michael's behavior was repulsive. Our daughter was an innocent girl and often felt lost and crossed about her father's wrongdoings. When depression came upon her, it was the final straw. Mercedes and I had independently chosen not to talk to Michael. Our daughter was well known for being extremely polite. Still, during the terrible times since we learned about Michaels's affair with Lina, Mercedes became cold, and her message toward Michael was unequivocal. I often caught her calling her father a douchebag when talking to friends. I knew she was agitated, and her opinion toward her father was clear. On several occasions, Michael pleaded for me to arrange for our her to share time with him, putting me in a difficult situation. How could I honestly suggest our daughter ignore the pain her father was causing her.

I tried to maintain peace between the three of us. Mercedes grew closer and closer to me, and that bothered Michael. We spoke about all sorts of things, tried to do our assignments together, went for walks, something to eat, to the gym and had coffee in our favorite places in Wanchai. Unfortunately, our apartment felt like a toxic chamber that strangled both of us. Often Mercedes asked me to sit on her bed while doing her homework. She would play classical or instrumental music, which she knows I like. My daughter would ask for baby time, consisting of her sitting on my lap and me holding her in my arms like a baby. She would ask questions, and I had to be honest, but the responses kept simple enough for a child to understand. My girl has contagious giggles, making me laugh every time she does. When I read in her room, she

CHAPTER 7: THE ABUSER

would put her stuffed animals next to me to keep me company while she was busy doing her homework. Sometimes, I caught her looking at me with her gorgeous big brown eyes while preparing paintbrushes before beginning a painting. I often wondered what was going on in her head. I miss those moments and hate that Michael stripped them from me in an attempt to destroy my relationship with our child.

In June 2017, there were three typhoons in four weeks in Hong Kong. It was amazing the amount of water that poured into the city. It looked like waterfalls all over, sometimes making it impossible to go outside. On one of those many muggy, rainy days, Mercedes asked me to swim with her; our building had an indoor pool. Michael became aware of the plan. He called me to the office and insisted I convince our daughter to let him join. Mercedes was not happy about it but didn't oppose either.

Our daughter was misinformed about the whole situation. Her mental health was fragile, and we needed to assess what bothered her or made her feel threatened. These were adult problems she couldn't understand. So, there were the three of us in the pool and a lonely lifeguard sitting in the far corner close to the big glass wall. After a while, Mercedes agreed that it was time to go home. A small waterfall divided the pool and locker rooms. Mercedes and I had two towels each to cover our wet hair. Michael realized he only had one. To protect his phone from getting wet, he entrusted it to Mercedes while the apparatus kept playing music.

When the truth is about to get revealed, it will, no matter what. We were changing, and a phone call interrupted the melody.

Mercedes clicked to accept the call; the woman replied, "Is it you, baby?"

I saw my daughter's face turn pale. The caller was Michael's mistress. I got extremely nervous, walked toward Mercedes and tried hugging her body, not yet fully dressed. She seemed distressed, grabbed a towel, phone in hand, and left in a hurry towards the elevator. Michael bumped into her as she was passing. I heard Mercedes screaming.

"You promised me, but you are a liar, I hate you."
Michael waited for me outside the locker room, asking what had happened.

"Your mistress is what happened," I said. "She called, and our daughter picked up."

At the apartment, Mercedes was waiting for us in our bedroom. It was surreal; she was sitting on our bed, in pajamas, her hair dripping wet, and Michael's mobile phone in her hand. As soon as she saw us, she said with teary eyes, "Can you please explain?"

I could see Michael having problems finding the words to reply. Mercedes kept the phone open, and when the three of us were ready to talk, she redialed.

Lina answered the phone, and we could hear on the speaker, "Hello, baby."

Our daughter replied, "Leave my family alone. I want you never to call again! Leave my family alone—I hate you!"

CHAPTER 7: THE ABUSER

Michael's mistress replied, "No, only if he asks me to do so."

Mercedes threw the phone at Michael and asked him to call back his bitch and ask her never to call him again.

"Please ask Lina to leave our family alone!"

Michael grabbed the phone and pretended to dial. He moved to an armchair in the corner of the room, close to the window and began typing. Michael was so into the message that he didn't realize I went and stood next to him. I grabbed the phone from his hands and read the note he was about to send.

"This number is not safe, don't use it again."

Wow! How low can a man get when in cheating mode. His daughter was crying in anguish, and all Michael could think was how to alert his hussy. Mercedes took the phone from my hand and ran to her bedroom, locking the door behind her. Michael followed her and threatened to knock down the door. He wanted his phone back. I knew how abusive Michael could get and worried for Mercedes. I thought about Michael's anger and desperation to recover his phone. The maternal instinct to protect a child defied the law of mass and size. I am 5'4, and at that time only weighed 43 kg. Michael is 6'2, weighing about 79 kg, but I still managed to put up a fight.

There was no way I would let Michael put his hand on our daughter. I asked her not to come out of the bedroom, no matter what. I got in between the door and Michael. He tried to push me around; he grabbed me by the neck and arms. He put his legs between my legs, trying to remove me from the door frame, but there was no way I was going to let him get close to Mercedes.

In August 2016, I had shoulder surgery. Unless I could stop Michael, he would target the injured arm. I ran towards my phone and did the only wise thing I could; I called for help by dialing the emergency number and requesting police assistance. It took a while for three police officers to arrive. A disgusting macho society in Hong Kong diminished the importance of my call. I got pushed aside, and the police addressed Michael first. One police officer directed me to the kitchen and blocked the doorway. The officers, with Michael, proceeded to take his statement. I could hear Michael giving his first and last name with the wrong spelling and telling them I was crazy and dangerous.

When the officers finished with Michael, one stayed with him, and a second one made his way to the kitchen to take my statement. Turning on all the lights in the kitchen, I showed the police my body covered in fresh bruises. I reminded them that I had called, not Michael. I expressed my fear and explained why Michael was so enraged. I emphasized my anxiety over Michael's typical aggressive behavior and his regular alcohol intoxication. I pointed out that our daughter had been the target of the fight and that I had no reason to believe that Michael would do the right thing if they let him stay.

The police asked if Michael was using drugs. I said that I had no idea, but he had done in the past. I requested the police officers to ask him to spend the night somewhere else. But Michael convinced the police that he was

CHAPTER 7: THE ABUSER

a powerful executive, and that the apartment lease was in his name. The police looked at me, then looked at Michael, and decided that there was a storm and that he could stay. The officers' "fabulous" solution was for the women to lock themselves in the primary bedroom until the next day. Mercedes preferred to remain in hers. It was an added torture, as I spent all night listening to any noise near her door.

After a long night, the morning light began to shine over the mountains of Mid-Levels East. I ran to my daughter's bedroom, but she was upset that I had called the police and chose not to speak to me. My body was in pain; I walked to Adventists Hospital, a few buildings down the road. As soon as the doctor saw me, he asked me to explain the bruises. He then prescribed sleeping medication and pills to help me control anxiety attacks and calm the pain. Next, the doctor suggested that I get a copy of the police report. After seeing the doctor, I made my way to the Happy Valley police station.

Hong Kong is not different from any other male-dominated society. I walked to the front desk and asked to speak to a police officer.

"Why?" the receptionist asked.

"Because I need a copy of my police report."

"You don't need that" he said.

"Yes, I do, sir."

Two other officers came to me and took me to a small room. The younger police officer spoke English well.

"Your name? Address?"

"Beautiful building" replied another police officer.

"Sorry lady, no report here."

"But sir, three police officers took statements last night."

"So, you called the police last night? About what?"

"My husband attacked me and threatened to force his way into my daughter's bedroom to hurt her."

To my surprise, the senior police officer asked me, "Why?"

"What do you mean, why?" I said.

He replied in his poor English, "Beating a wife is not a crime."

Sadly enough, the young police officer told me that there were many cases in which husbands beat up their wives. Such incidents don't get reported as urgent matters since they are family "arguments". It is pathetic to read in newspapers how one of the wealthiest countries in the world constantly fails to protect children and women from abuse.

Despite the officers' opinions that my matter lacked importance, I insisted that I would report what had happened last night if there was no report. Police officers kept asking me what I wanted to do with the report. I felt as if they somehow wanted to protect the perpetrator. In the end, I was promised a report number within the next week or so.

Unfortunately, all I received that day was a reference number, which turned out to be useless. Despite my several attempts to obtain the report, I never got one. Two years later, after the incident, and to back up my arguments in London, I hired a solicitor in Hong Kong to investigate the matter. A reply from Happy Valley Police appeared. It had wrong names, dates, and a lack of details, making my efforts futile.

Bewildered and Sad

Despite all the distractions and problems at home, Mercedes completed her International Baccalaureate. She was nothing less than a champion after the hard work and the brutal circumstances at home. The informal graduation party was to take place in an area called Lan Kwai Fong in the central region of Hong Kong Island. Fortunately, planning the details of the party took her attention from the issues she was experiencing at home. I was distributing coffee in Central and found Mercedes as she walked to meet her friend before heading to the party. She looked pretty; I noticed her skirt was short, but I didn't say anything. She was heading to a party and I didn't want to ruin the good mood. I asked if she had enough money or if I should give her some.

Mercedes said, "Dad gave me some, so for now, this girl is loaded with cash!"

I headed home, and when I saw Michael, I asked when our daughter was supposed to get back home.

"I didn't set a time for her to come home, he replied."

"But Michael, how could you? Our daughter is heading to an area full of bars, dubious men, wearing a tiny skirt and loaded with cash; it's not a place for her to be hanging around late at night!"

"So, what do you want, Diana? That was the place chosen for the kids to have fun. I trust they will hang around together, and everything will be fine. It's her graduation party; let her enjoy it."

I said no more, but I could not stop worrying for some reason.

At 11:30 p.m. I called Mercedes to check on her, but she did not answer; so, Michael began calling as well. Finally, I proposed to make our way to Lan Kwai Fong if we didn't hear from our daughter by midnight. Well, midnight passed, and there was no sign of Mercedes. Michael didn't seem in a rush to head to Central. I became impatient and went to the bedroom to get dressed to go by myself. Suddenly, I heard Michael putting on his shoes in a hurry. Rather than calling the intercom, the concierge desk had called Michael's mobile phone.

"What's going on?"

"Nothing, go to sleep" Michael said. "Everything is fine. I need to go downstairs and pay for Mercedes' taxi fare."

But she had money; what happened? Michael took the elevator without saying another word. I went back to the bedroom to grab more cash just in case. I heard the voices of several people, then ran to the living room; I saw the light in Mercedes' bathroom. A female voice said,

"Please get me some water."

I saw my daughter unconscious on the bathroom floor; her friend Rachel was kneeling next to her.

"What happened to Mer?" I asked her friend.

CHAPTER 7: THE ABUSER

I urged Michael to take our daughter to hospital; the child was not well. My daughter's lips were starting to get blue. She had greenish, yellowish vomit all over her clothes. Michael was trying to wash her face. I knew that Michael was not reacting fast enough. And Merce's life was in danger.

"What's wrong with you, Michael!"

"Get out; this is not about you!" he yelled back.

"Michael, take my daughter to the hospital right now, or I will call an ambulance and the police."

I began filming to put pressure on him. "Take her to the hospital right now!"

The bastard did not want to take our daughter to the hospital because he was afraid of a social worker investigating the reasons behind whatever happened to Mercedes. Imagine how twisted and selfish that man is. He finally called the concierge for a taxi. I went to the bedroom to grab my purse.

"You are not coming" he said. "Only Rachel and I will go. Rachel speaks Cantonese and can help; you are useless."

"Fuck you, Michael. I am coming because I need to make sure my daughter is fine."

He rushed down the elevator leaving me behind. I took the service elevator, and when I realized the taxi was going without me, Michael was holding the door shut from inside. I ran and got in front of the cab, and the driver allowed me to jump in the front seat.

Our daughter was taken directly into the ER. One of the doctors asked for a summary of what had happened.

Michael asked Rachel to speak with the doctor in Cantonese.

"No way" I said. "Doctor, you speak English, right?"
"Yes."

"OK, Rachel, could you please explain in English."

It turned out that the big group split into small groups after a few hours, and a group of girls, including Mercedes, wanted to keep dancing and jumped from bar to bar to find the best atmosphere. At the last bar, Mercedes insisted on staying at the table. When the rest of the girls returned, our daughter was rolling her eyes and almost unresponsive. Instead of taking Mercedes to the hospital, they panicked and decided to drag her to a taxi, and only Rachel accompanied her home. She was vomiting a yellow substance.

"I got afraid Mercedes would choke" her friend said.
The doctor asked many other questions, but Rachel was unsure what Mercedes drank. Finally, I got Rachel to tell me more of what she witnessed that night. At first, she mentioned that Mercedes was absent through the night. As the time passed, she confessed feeling heartbroken and kept saying that all she wanted was her family back. The horrible pain Michael and I brought to our children is something that will haunt me for the rest of my life, and I feel deeply sorry for that.

It was horrendous to see my daughter in such a state. She was unresponsive and pale. The doctors couldn't do much besides bodily fluid samples, which they sent for urgent analysis. Mercedes was in such a bad condition;

CHAPTER 7: THE ABUSER

doctors were afraid of even putting intravenous to hydrate her for fear of adverse reactions. The risk of choking was a big concern. The two doctors didn't leave Mercedes for one second. They asked Michael and me to speak to her as much as possible. We began to place ice cubes on her forehead, hands and legs. I rubbed her feet and told her stories of funny things she had done. The doctors wanted her to show signs of consciousness. The lab results finally came in. Mercedes had a significant amount of methanol in her body. Every second, Mercedes was unresponsive, it felt eternal. I thought about my children and how much I loved them. I remember when I first saw my children after labor and their first cry. I wanted to give Mercedes my life. I prayed with all my heart. I knew Mercedes was born with a purpose.

"Please, God, watch after this angel. You are in command."

Finally, Mercedes moved her leg a touch. Michael and I began talking to her, rubbing her legs and hands.

"Sweetheart, please open your eyes. Do you hear us? Open your eyes. Can you move your hand?"

As soon as she moved her lips, doctors and nurses took over. Michael and I stepped aside. Our daughter spoke incoherently, but it was enough for the doctors to give her an injection to help neutralize some of the poison in her system. A few hours later, she became stable and was transferred to a room. Michael and I sat on opposite sides of her bed.

After some time, Michael left the room without saying a word. He returned to the hospital about an hour later. Michael had gone home to collect Mercedes' favorite stuffed animal. When he returned, he put it on our daughter's arm. Then, he got close to me and told me he had called Lina.

"I wanted to tell her about what Mercedes did. I don't want anything to do with her anymore. Do you know what she told me? She told me that I was selfish."

"Michael, I couldn't care less what Lina told you. All I know is that our child almost died. So, right now, you and Lina are not my priority."

Joy came to my life when Mercedes was discharged and sent home. Michael tried to convince one of the doctors not to record the poison because she may get in trouble at school. The hospital is private, and doctors were more flexible, but they refused to lie for Michael. So, the doctor wrote a note for our daughter to get excused several days from school to recover after not feeling well.

After Mercedes came home, I could not bear to be in the apartment. The shock of all the anxiety and depression took a toll on me. I tried to hide it by asking the helper to check on my daughter while taking short walks. On one occasion, Michael saw me leaving and asked me if he could join. In the beginning, we walked, then jogged. When I was in good health, I was as fast as Michael. But, back then, I was fragile and could not keep up. Before the running path ended and forked into two longer tracks, I decided to stop and walk back home. Michael told me that he was not ready to stop running and will stay behind. I turned around and began fast walking back home. A few minutes into the walk, I heard that unique voice, clear and

CHAPTER 7: THE ABUSER

robust again. "Follow him...run!" This time, I turned around immediately and without hesitation, I began running in the direction Michael was heading. Finally, I got to the first section of the trail. The flat part of the path ended, and a slippery, steep strip began. I was almost out of oxygen but kept going and ended up at the top, where a road splits the mountain. I crossed the road and took a break.

Michael and I had run up that mountain many times before. At one point, the path forks in two different directions. One side goes to the East, ending close to the French International School of Hong Kong in Happy Valley. The other takes to the South-West of the island toward Tai Tam reservoir and high into the mountains. When I got to the fork, I asked, "Please tell me which way?" This time, there was no voice, but I knew it was on the left. So, I steered left and kept running. In the distance, I could see Michael's orange jersey. Thank you! I kept running as fast as I could to catch up with him. For what, I had no idea. All I knew was that I had to get close to him.

My heartbeats were very fast, so I began walking before reaching Michael. A group of hikers passed next to him; they were chatting and laughing. Michael didn't hear me getting close, about three feet behind him. I could overhear his conversation with Lina. He was reassuring her that he was not sleeping with me.

"I know how to handle the situation" he said.

I tapped Michael's shoulder. He saw me and raised the hand holding the phone while removing his headphones with the other. He had the phone high and pressed for the phone to shut down.

"Hello Michael, who was the person on the phone?"

"No one, I was listening to music, but something went wrong. So, I need to reset the phone."

It was June 2017 and Father's Day was approaching. I remarked on that and mentioned that Mercedes had asked me what to do to celebrate.

Michael said, "Diana, weren't you feeling weak and heading back home? Why are you following me?"

"Well, Michael, in the beginning, I was not sure why, but now I know."

Michael mocked me and said, "You wanted to run, so let's go."

"OK, Michael, you lead."

He ran fast, and I was next to him. I couldn't breathe and, at one point, felt as if having a heart attack, but I didn't stop until we got home. The two of us headed to our bedroom. Before showering, I asked Michael to show me his phone with recent phone calls. He began screaming, and our daughter came to the second floor. She asked, what was going on?

"Nothing," Michael said. "It's your crazy mother, she wants to see my phone."

Mercedes said, "So what is the problem?"

"I have not received any call from Lina, and she thinks I did."

"Dad, you wouldn't lie to me, right?" our daughter said.

"Of course, not".

CHAPTER 7: THE ABUSER

"OK, Dad, then let me see your phone."

Michael ran to the bathroom and, behaving like a child, locked the door. A few minutes later, he came out with his phone in hand.

"Here's my phone; you two are crazy. Inspect my phone, it's open, check all you want!"

"I really don't care anymore" I replied.

Mercedes took his phone and looked at the recent phone calls.

"What is this, Dad? You don't have any phone calls since yesterday. What about the phone call you received from the dry cleaners this morning? It's not here. Did you delete all your calls? Why? Who called you this morning? Who was it, Dad?"

Michael refused to tell the truth and began a fight with me.

"Diana, look what you have done; you are horrible; you don't care about our daughter!"

Until today, I admire my daughter for being so bold and brave.

Shannon Thomas,[11] a therapist once wrote, "Toxic people project their own character defects onto their victims. They do this by accusing the victim of the exact actions they themselves do but deny."[12]

Dr. Zaidi

Hours became days, days became weeks, and Mercedes and I continued to be trapped in a toxic situation, not knowing how to escape. She needed a child psychologist; Michael and I undoubtedly did too. Finally, a child psychologist came well recommended, and Mercedes began sessions. It's still painful to remember my girl also experiencing anxiety attacks and much sadness at her young age. She began writing about all the good and not-so-good feelings and things happening to her daily. The content of their meetings is kept confidential unless absolutely necessary to release details. It was essential for the psychologist to gain Mercedes' trust and for our daughter to have someone she could confide in.

I began looking for another couple's therapist to help Michael and me handle the hell we were living. After an extensive search, and among the top ones, a doctor from England showed up with 20 years of experience, an impeccable reputation, and credentials. I called to book an appointment.

The receptionist replied, "Madam, Dr. Zaidi, is traveling, and her calendar will be fully booked for weeks to come."

Deep inside, I knew Dr. Zaidi was the right therapist. There are times when "No" is not the correct answer.

At around 5 p.m. I called again and a different voice answered. I asked if I leave an urgent message for Dr. Zaidi, and said it was very important.

"I am Dr. Zaidi" the lady replied, "What is the emergency?",

"I thought you were on a business trip" I said.

"I arrived today—I have so much work that I need to get ready for tomorrow."

CHAPTER 7: THE ABUSER

"Please make a space in your calendar for my matter; it's complicated and has delicate issues that need immediate attention."

"Call tomorrow; my assistant will provide an appointment."

Dr. Zaidi came into my life as if she was an angel. Now it was up to me to convince Michael to keep the appointment. The task was not easy, but eventually, he agreed.

Michael and I were to buy a book related to infidelity, read it and discuss it during therapy sessions. Reading the book was like reliving what Michael had done to me. Every step of the book's exhibits and descriptions were an exact mirror of his actions. Had Michael previously bought the textbook to learn how to commit the "perfect" crime? Or was he told how to do it? When I asked Dr. Zaidi about the coincidence, she told me that all unfaithful partners usually follow the same pattern.

"So, there is a guide for cheaters?"

"No" she replied, "It is that evil minds think alike".

I knew an expert in the field. It was Lina.

Michael and I received assignments to complete at home before our next appointment. We were supposed to take notes and see how we progressed. Sometimes Michael and I would sit next to our bed facing the big window looking over Victoria Harbor, chat on a friendly basis and discuss our situation. Sometimes we talk about fun things, the news of our children, or our anniversary that just had passed; sometimes we hugged, and other times we cried.

When the time came to return to couples therapy, Michael would become a completely different person. Most of the time, he would request that I speak first. Then, he would contradict every point I made.

"No, Dr. Zaidi, we never speak friendly. We never sit together. We never hug. We never smile. There are no good memories. I don't understand why Diana lies."

I would look at the therapist, and the therapist looked at me and then at Michael. She had found something in Michael's eyes. Dr. Zaidi knew how to read him. She knew when Michael was not sincere. It was a total mockery and waste of time. After every appointment, Mercedes would ask how the session went. All I could say was that it was a work in progress.

Living with Michael was like being with Dr. Jekyll and Hyde. He put in practice mental torture on me. Michael stopped sleeping in the guest bedroom and forced his way to the main bedroom where I slept. I was not allowed to leave either. If I tried to sneak out at night to sleep somewhere else, he would drag me back. I had made it clear to Michael that I wanted the divorce. He is a lousy loser, and even if he had his mistress between his eyes, he had no guts to accept rejection.

I knew our relationship was over, especially after what happened to our daughter and the pain I felt went I saw her at the hospital—the lack of concern from Michael created fear and uncertainty about what was to come. Michael had terrorized my life for too long, and it was enough. I wanted no more. I was afraid to have lost what it took to remain strong. As a result, my mind and body

CHAPTER 7: THE ABUSER

will often get paralyzed, and nightmares invade most of the time when I close my eyes. Michael hated me for calling the divorce. It was a blow to his ego, turning me into his number one enemy.

Michael would suggest that I commit suicide. Then, before bed, he would read books aloud about heartbroken partners who committed suicide. He made me watch depressing films or buy books with stories of tragedy and death, including the killings of Pedro Escobar. I endured Michael's sadistic behavior for months. My mental state was fragile. I didn't know how to make him stop. Finally, I told Dr. Zaidi about it. Together we confronted Michael, but he was way ahead of the game with plans I couldn't even imagine at that time.

Michael was behind my back, looking for a job abroad. In August, he got an interview and told me a few days before he traveled. Michael was ready to abandon Mercedes and me in Hong Kong and move on. I asked why he waited a few days before the trip to tell me. He told me that I was lucky.

"Stein told me not to say anything until after I was gone. I do not want you to follow me; I need to take precautions."

Michael's traveling date came. Before leaving for the airport, he changed our safe box's access code. Mercedes and my passport, along with other vital documents locked inside. The following day, Michael called. I asked why he changed the combination code of our safe.

"I didn't want to see you in London", he replied.

"Me following you, Michael? You are hallucinating, darling."

I wished him luck with the job interview and ended the call. Once a strong woman, I could now see myself in the mirror fading away.

A week or so after Michael's interview, a package of private and confidential documents came via messenger. Michael found the envelope in the office and screamed with joy.

"I cannot believe how lucky I am; I got the job! I am moving to London!"

We were in a middle of a huge typhoon. The building was swaying. I was constantly dizzy. My blood pressure was high, causing tension in my ears and obstructing hearing. I witnessed Michael's excitement, and then I don't remember how I ended up in the parking lot located on the third floor of the building. I was in shock and crying inconsolably. I guess because I didn't know what else to do.

I asked myself what would happen to Mercedes and me. What do I do to get a divorce if Michael is soon gone? Mercedes came to find me. The sky was surreal with gorgeous grey, yellow and blue tones. There were puffy and stratus clouds mixed and moving fast.

"Look at the sky" I said, wiping my eyes.

She sat in an area where we could see the sky and asked me to take a couple of pictures; she wore a deep pink scarf and looked beautiful. I asked her to stay with me for a while. Trying to console me, Mercedes repeated what her psychologist had told her before. The wind gained

CHAPTER 7: THE ABUSER

force, and one of the security guards asked us to return to our flat.

"It's dangerous" he said.

As we walked toward the elevator, the wind made an eerie noise as it zigzagged the pillars of the structure. Mercedes and I returned home and saw Michael with the biggest smile. I wanted the divorce; why did I feel so sad? Perhaps because we were married and nothing had legally concluded, I was like a soul in limbo. No purpose and I couldn't see my future. After Michael received the job offer, he decided to travel alone to the property in Guatemala, claiming he needed a vacation. The irony of Michael heading to the place once held with hope and dreams for our family. The same house I helped salvage from construction disasters. The same house I helped salvage from construction disasters. I requested my elder brother to collect mom and my sister Flory from the place in Antigua and take them to his home in the city for a week. Except for my two brothers, the rest of my family was unaware of my marital problems. Silly me. I thought I could keep it to myself until it was time to announce the divorce. During Michael's stay at the property, I saw him in the surveying cameras walking back and forth in the corridors. Sometimes, he will call me from the house as we usually did before and ask me to look at the cameras to wave goodbye on his way out. I felt as if we were living in an alternative reality. So many things were crumbling, and there it was, Michael pretending all was fine; I guess for him, it was.

Unfortunately, while Michael was away, Mercedes got ill. Neither she nor the helper was allowed to collect the prescribed medicine. So, after doing my rounds visiting clients and distributing coffee, I stopped at the hospital for the prescription. Multiple typhoons and humidity left walkways slippery and with dark, green moss. The Adventist Hospital is on a hill, very close to our building.

I saw a taxi at the front door when I left the hospital but decided to walk to save the fare. Crossing the pedestrian path, I slipped. I felt awkwardly twisting my right foot and leg, trying to protect my right shoulder because of the recent surgery. In seconds, I felt an excruciating pain in my ankle and shin. The pain was such that it made me vomit. Afraid of fainting, I began to scream for help. It was close to 6:00 p.m. getting dark, and the foot traffic to and from the hospital had stopped. I dragged myself to the nearest handrail and was able to stand. I saw a driver sitting in his parked car. I screamed, but he did not hear me. I managed to get close to the door and tapped the window. He opened it; I asked for help.

"Emergency!" I cried.

The driver closed the window and continued reading his newspaper. I felt that I had only a bit more strength, and when I began to faint, I unwillingly put my injured foot on the ground and heard my bone crack.

"NO!! Please, help!"

I noticed a woman walking down the hill towards me. When she saw me in distress, she ran back to the checkpoint about 30 meters away and called for help. A nurse came with a wheelchair and took me to the emergency room. My trousers were cut into pieces and sent for X-rays. My foot was very swollen, my ankle turned into a huge red purplish ball, and my shin was bleeding. I had dislocated my ankle and fractured my fibula. The doctor was concerned about the position of the bone and ordered immediate surgery. Meantime, I received an injection for the pain, which did very little to help. I called the house, spoke to Mercedes, briefly explained my situation and asked her to send our helper with my medical insurance card. I pleaded with the surgeon not to operate; I needed to talk to Michael first.

I called Michael and told him about the accident.

"Please make sure you do not consent to surgery. I want you to know that I disapprove of it. I need you to please communicate that to the doctors."

I was about to pass out from the pain. I knew that I would not come back if I got under anesthesia. The superhuman strength inside me kept me from fading until Michael said

"OK, let me talk to the doctors."

After that, I don't remember anything else. I woke up in the hospital bed.

The bone expert called a team of surgeons to talk to me and explain their opinion. Madam, our immediate reaction would have been to operate and place the fibula in place with a wire. Unfortunately, your leg is weak, and the crack in the bone is long and deep. But we have agreed to immobilize the leg with a cast and give you a week until a subsequent X-ray. If we don't see the tiniest improvement, we will remove the cast and perform surgery.

Lucky for me, we started to see tiny improvements the following week. For one month, I got X-rays over the cast every week. After that, the cast and I became good companions. I named it "Blackbird." I took him for walks, and we learned how to carry coffee samples by train, bus and taxi. We even rode in electrical escalators with the help of crutches. Blackbird and I used to sleep together and take showers together, he wore a plastic cape, I did not. After long months of Blackbird and me, my bones healed, and I had to say goodbye. But not before taking pictures of him before and after leaving my leg.

Physio was painful, and on the first day, I cried because I didn't want to put my foot on the ground. I begged for my crutches until I got them back. I got told by the doctors that my brain remembered the injury and kept me from willingly putting my foot on the floor. Practice, practice, and more practice led me to walk ultimately without any aid. As soon as I was able, I went for short and then long walks until I could gently jog, and much later, run again. By 2021, I was back to my usual 5 km run twice a week.

Chapter 8

Goodbye Michael

In mid-September 2017, after accepting the job with Capula Investments in London as Chief Risk Officer, Michael hired a removal company we used before called AGS. The company came to our home and packed all his belongings into two shipments, one by plane and the other by sea. First, they took art pieces including one that means a lot to me. I made it when Mercedes was about six-years-old. Then Michael instructed the removal people to pack all his books, bank statements, recent tax documents, and practically everything he could grab except the furniture and the printer in the office.

Luckily for me, Michael forgot that I was responsible for maintaining the filing of our personal affairs. I had two other sources where I file items that we constantly access for reference and old files in boxes in the storage room where I kept my stock of coffee beans. Michael had taken multiple file boxes to AMP Credit Technology, anticipating his departure from Hong Kong. Among those boxes was the cherished box labeled "AIG". The content documents taken from AIG in the US and London offices. Inside were memos, internal correspondence letters, documents, transactions, information about different trades, and practically all kinds of privileged documents that should have never left AIG. I never paid attention to the extent of the content, until Michael got boxes ready to take to AMP.

I recall asking Michael a couple of times why we didn't move some of the boxes with old records to the storage room. He replied with a resounding "No, don't you dare". Those are documents with valuable information I need in the lawsuit against AIG. He had failed in his lawsuit against AIG Financial Products Corp. in the US, and now unilaterally decided to join a group with other ex-colleagues from AIG London, to launch a case against AIG UK.

He is a person who doesn't take losing very well. So, it was a matter of ego to continue with the fight. Among the group launching the lawsuit was his friend, ex-colleague and owner of My Community Bank and Gojoko both UK-based companies. As far as I learned from Michael back in 2017, My Community Bank is a lending entity that grew from a former credit union, and Gojoko is the loan processor, with integrated risk management and data analytics. Michael was the instrumental piece linking these companies with AMP Credit Technology in Hong Kong. But not without first investing our family

CHAPTER 8: GOODBYE MICHAEL

money in the three companies. He was to benefit from the corporate union in a very rewarding manner. Meantime, Michael was very much on the way to spending our money including about $300,000 USD which ended up down the drain in litigation proceedings between 2016 and 2020 in his lawsuit against AIG UK. I objected several times when I noticed bills coming in and the money put aside in Therium; a company to set money aside for litigations. But Michael being a financial savvy investor decided to gamble our money on a hopeless cause, losing the litigation on 6 August 2020 due to a lack of arguable point of law. The Supreme Court of the United Kingdom refused further permission to appeal.

During our divorce proceedings in London, Michael had to turn over all credit card and bank statements. I noticed that he had rented a storage room near his place in Marylebone. As I said before, he is a very paranoid person, and perhaps he didn't want to have any of the incriminating records with him. In court, I had made clear my claims of physical abuse. Unfortunately for me, Michael was aware that I knew too much. It was a matter of principle, so as soon as I could, contacted the offices of AIG in London.

The next step was to try Connecticut, US. I'm not sure how, and with one call, I got directed to one of the key people in the investment and trading departments. It was my opportunity to let them know about the records. I became fully aware of the documents and could not keep the detail to myself. Since the lawsuit was against AIG London, I mentioned contacting the London office. I told him about the box with records; I also shared the storage room details. The gentleman took note of everything we exchanged contact information. And after that, we never spoke again. It was now up to them to do whatever they felt necessary.

In his last attempt to help him deem me insane, Michael sought one last in-person appointment with Dr. Zaidi. He requested to exclude me from the session. After that meeting, I insisted on an in-person couples' meeting. Dr. Zaidi asked Michael what he wanted to do about the treatment and sessions. Michael had agreed to help us get to a point we could talk amicably about separation, perhaps divorce. But, I think guilt hunted him, and he insisted on keeping up with the sessions and somehow mending our relationship. He chose to continue with the sessions via Skype. No one was forcing Michael to continue with the treatments. He was heading to London and didn't even have to see my face anymore. I felt lost and confused, and most of the time followed whatever just to keep some peace around Mercedes and me.

Feeling somehow relieved, deep inside, I was hopeful that Michael would have a good sense of right and wrong, and eventually take care of his family. Dr. Zaidi strongly advised me to arrange weekly sessions with modules containing alternative support for my personal needs. In November, I learned that Dr. Zaidi already knew about the outcome of my relationship with Michael. Even well-trained experts must have a hard time knowing a drowning patient's situation will soon worsen.

CHAPTER 8: GOODBYE MICHAEL

Toward the end of October 2017, Michael called me with a cry for help. At Capula Investments, he passed as a respectable family man, whose family was left behind in Hong Kong because of his daughter's school. The partners and high-up management began to wonder where his wife was. Why wasn't I visiting Michael in London? To top it all, one of the partners had set up a dinner and private viewing of an art exhibit at Somerset House. Apparently, he wanted to meet me there. In a panic, Michael called me and requested the favor to accompany him.

I was walking on crutches and still in pain from my fall. But the first thing Michael asked was if I could dress elegantly and not use crutches. I told him that I wasn't sure but would see what I could do. I had no intention of harming anyone and decided to help in whichever possible way. When I arrived in London, Michael waited for me at the airport. When Michael needs something, he prostitutes himself, doing anything to get what he wants. He was greedy and made me stay in his Marylebone apartment.

Previously, Michael had bitterly complained that the company apartment provided was in an area where his colleagues could often see him, hence moving to a flat in Marylebone. How bad could it have been, Michael? It was Mayfair. But there is no reasoning with him, especially when he doesn't share his whole plan. Not long after, I understood that his plan was to bring prostitutes to the apartment and eventually his mistress. The ground-floor apartment could not have been more hidden. It was located in a dark alley behind a strip of buildings backside the main street, in a passageway leading to three different roads.

Two days before the event at the museum, Michael insisted on meeting at a sophisticated restaurant in Mayfair, London. The way he set things up left me feeling uneasy. First, he asked me to meet him for a drink; then, he introduced me to his ex-colleague from the Symmetry London office. He instructed me to leave after a quick introduction as he was to stay and have dinner with this man. I met Michael on the specified evening. While chatting, I asked why he would want me to meet these men and not stay for dinner. Michael replied that it was a bit complicated.

"I will try to snatch this man from Symmetry and lure him to work under me in Capula."

Upset about the reason given, I asked why he needed me there.

His bold response was: "I seem respectable and solid with you by my side. So far, we have been a power couple; without you, many things could have never happened. You made us look good, and I need this guy to feel confident with what I am about to propose."

Afraid to say no, and feeling like I had no choice, I followed along.

When Michael got dismissed from Symmetry Investments in Hong Kong, I joined him to review "Terms of Separation" before taking them to his employment lawyers. Among the "must not do" items on the list, it was forbidden for Michael to hire or compel any Symmetry employees from leaving the company. In one of his

CHAPTER 8: GOODBYE MICHAEL

vengeful attacks, Michael had already persuaded Gareth M., a top IT person, to resign after he got dismissed from Symmetry. And here was Michael again, doing precisely what he was forbidden. After meeting with his ex-colleague, Michael returned home, disappointed that the guy refused his glamourous offer; he was too loyal. In silence, I rejoiced!

It is the night of the event at Somerset House; throughout my life, for good or for bad, I have always felt comfortable with people from all walks of life. All eyes were on me. I kept my composure but could not stop feeling guilty for allowing Michael to use me as an instrument of deception. I clicked well with two of the main three partners. The wife of one of them was an eccentric Asian woman shamelessly walking around and gazing at me from head to toe. While I looked at her movements from the corner of my eye, I could not stop wondering what she wanted to see. She didn't even bother to say hello. Her husband sat to my left; one other partner sat to my right and at the head of the table.

Michael was seated in the extremely far corner of the long, beautifully decorated table next to the wife of the company partner to my right. Michael seemed nervous, and his head constantly turned toward me. Perhaps wondering what was I talking about? What was so funny that made others laugh? At one point, he couldn't resist and walked to my seat and asked if everything was all right.

"Hey honey, how are my bosses treating you? You are only telling good stories about me, right?"

"Oh, I didn't know there were bad ones. If they are, I leave it up to you to amuse the crowd", I replied. "Don't worry, this girl is in good hands."

He looked at me with pleading eyes as if imploring, "Please, woman, don't you dare fuck this one up."

It was clear that I had accepted the task, and no way would I change my mind. Honor and loyalty are scarce commodities.

One of the partners mentioned his son had gone to Costa Rica to study Spanish. I gave him insights about Guatemala and the tumultuous history of Central America and the civil wars. To what he commented, not knowing much about. I referred to parts of Bitter Fruit's comprehensive book with factual information about the subject. I promised to send him a copy in English, which I sourced and later shipped from Hong Kong. This triggered a lengthy conversation and made the night quite fun. Having lived short but engaging experiences in Hong Kong led me to think about how far the United States of America is from the mark. Despite their proximity to Latin America, great opportunities have gone unappreciated. I feel that the USA works hard to dominate and oppress Latin American countries. Just imagine where all the USA-prohibited pesticides and chemicals end up. If you guessed Central, South America and the Caribbean, you guessed right. In the meantime, China is gaining territory in Brazil, Chile, and Ecuador, to mention some, by taking advantage of their natural resources, mining, and even learning agronomy from Chile. In addition, China has

CHAPTER 8: GOODBYE MICHAEL

offered an open bridge between some countries with mutual work and study opportunities. Meanwhile, the USA is still dealing with the challenge of knowing its country's name and calling itself America and its inhabitants Americans. They do not yet recognize that they are only part of a vast continent.

The Partner's wife (whom we'll call Sue), came around, held my shoulders, and briefly joined the conversation. From the side of my left eye, I could see that made Michael even more uncomfortable. We agreed with Sue to stay in touch, which I never mentioned to Michael. So, no one could ever say that I didn't try to help uncover the corrupt and false person they had in their hands. Later in the book, I hope to help you understand the statement I just made.

After the gathering at the museum, Michael became an argumentative, judgmental malicious old self. In the short time I stayed with Michael in London, he controlled even the money I spent to buy groceries to cook his meals and cleaning supplies to scrub his place. Stingy and cruel, despite having just received £200,00 GBP as a joining bonus the month before. A few nights prior to my return to Hong Kong, I made Michael his favorite stew, prepared the table and waited for him to have dinner. Instead of talking about the mess we were in, he began bragging at about taking his team to the best restaurants and bars for the pre-official company holiday party. I could not hold it in and asked whether the company would pay for that.

"Of course, not", he replied. "The outings are on me".

"But you keep telling me that there is no money", I said.

A stream of criticism poured and heard it was me the selfish one.

"I will be doing that for the whole family's benefit. I need to set a strong presence among my team; don't you see it?"

Finally, I could not take it anymore. Hypocrisy was too much to bear. I grabbed a phone, called my friend, took the crutches and my luggage and left his apartment. While waiting for my friend to collect me so I could spend the night with her, I stood in the cold, crying on the grounds of a church. A young girl passing by approached me and asked if I was alright; she offered the juice bottle from her hand. Without knowing it, she had given me the strength I needed. After that, I could not put up the show again.

My son David accompanied me two days later to the divorce lawyer for the first consultation. Since I discovered Michael's affair, a family friend and lawyer herself recommended a divorce solicitor in London. I went to the first appointment with very little money for the consultation, a Sapphire bracelet given to me by Michael the year before for my birthday. I couldn't explain how humiliated I felt. Michael's words came like a dagger stabbing hard,

"Enjoy this bracelet. It would be good in case of emergency if you need money in a hurry."

Little did I know in March 2016 that I would ever need to sell the only luxury piece of jewelry he bought for me.

CHAPTER 8: GOODBYE MICHAEL

The legal firm was Anthony Gold. I returned to Hong Kong, and Michael was served to initiate divorce in November 2017. My story with Anthony Gold goes beyond what I ever imagined. We will return to this legal firm towards the end of my book. When I found myself alone, down, and on my knees, I encountered people waiting in line to take a shot at me in an attempt to make my miserable situation worse. What these cowards don't know is that victims remember who they are. If the ordeal is survived, we will only get stronger, coming back, slowly but surely, to put things right.

Chapter 9

The Legal Firms

As my life began to crumble, I went into emergency mode, asking for advice and reaching out to friends. Some remained faithful to our friendship; others showed their authentic selves and told me not to call; some ran away as if I was fire. It was hard to understand why they were being so cruel; I guess such is a human reaction when in selfish mode.

Camilla Fusco and Anthony Gold Solicitors

I had to borrow a small amount of money from a friend in Hong Kong to pay for Camilla's initial consultation; when we first met, I felt broken and fearful for my future. I knew what Michael could do when angry and in a fight. So, I urged her to tread with caution when it came to Michael. Camilla quizzed me for sources of cash. Her questions made me remember a modest IRA deposit, which helped pay some of Camilla's bills. She was interested in all assets such as homes, stocks, shares, savings, pension plans, everything. She asked for an approximate amount of Michael's earnings and where he worked, to the point of googling the company. No marital home? I said that we used to have a townhouse in New York City but sold it in 2014. I was keen to purchase a property in London, but I couldn't convince Michael to invest. I mentioned his company in Hong Kong and the company in Guatemala, to which I was a shareholder. I remember telling Camila that once my company in Hong Kong matured, it would help store grains. It would also serve as a distribution hub for farmers in the highlands of Guatemala to drop their grain before arranging export.

"So, the property is in a trust?"

"No", I said, "It's an asset to the company. I don't want to disclose it because it is not mine, there are other shareholders involved, and Michael is a monster; he plays dirty, and I am afraid of him."

Camilla insisted that I had to put forward the property in the report. I insisted that it was a company. She then said, if you have more shares, it must be like it is in Italy; the company's interest is solely yours. I had no idea of Italian law but insisted that the issue was complicated and urged Camilla to speak with the Guatemalan corporate lawyer. In reality, she needed to report my participation in a company and specify my shares so it could be tangible the existence of a company rather than a house. But, she didn't want to listen or try to understand what I

CHAPTER 9: THE LEGAL FIRMS

was explaining. Instead, she took a firm tone by saying that I had to look for another solicitor if I did not follow her advice. I insisted on not having enough time to source another solicitor. She knew I was travelling back to Hong Kong the following day.

"Are you sure, Camilla, that what you are telling me is correct?"

She replied positively. She also required several blank pages with my signature; not confident why, but I was desperate and agreed. I also signed the contract, hence assigning Camilla to defend my side.

Little did I know that Camilla's insisting on the property in Guatemala and her actions would mess up my case. Instead of believing in her client, she took a blind path to litigate against a liar, cheater and controlling adversary. I found Camilla's approach in my proceedings a total failure. It seemed like she was taking orders from the other party's solicitors instead of looking out for my best interest. Moreover, she was of inferior pedigree to Michael's solicitors. And the differences became apparent in her handling of my case.

My request for her to manage my matter more aggressively went unheard. For me, it was difficult to concentrate on so many things at once. I kept getting attacked by all sides, and Michael was doing his best to see me jump off a bridge. Behind my back, he was luring our daughter to move to a separate apartment and leave the family home. He knew I was strict with our daughter, and she wanted to go offline and spend time with her boyfriend and allow him at home when I was not around. I noticed several emails where Michael would send rental options in the area to tempt her. He was quick to ignore me when I sought his help regarding our daughter's behavior since December 2017. Michael twisted my concerns for Mercedes's well-being, making me look like the bad guy. And he decided to take advantage of the situation and orchestrated friction between our child and me. We got to a point when she left the family apartment with her boyfriend and did not return until late that night. In a panic, I called her brothers on another continent to help me locate her. Two days after the incident, Michael touched down in Hong Kong, falsely claiming that our daughter was mistreated and abused. He transferred our daughter to a service apartment and denied me knowledge of where she was. It was agony, to the point that I had to go to her school and request help. But Michael is a talker, and soon after, I was seen as the crazy one.

I contacted Camilla and asked for help, and was told that a 14-year-old teenager is considered an adult in Hong Kong. My guess is that Michael knew that. I could not get my daughter to come back, and he didn't want to tell me where Mercedes was. Then, while running an errand in an area called Happy Valley, I saw them walking near me. They were laughing. It is inexplicable how they did not see me, I felt as if I was in the twilight zone. At least I knew she was fine.

The next day, 5 February, Michael marched into the apartment with two men from the AGS removal company and one of his ex-colleagues named Gareth from Symmetry Investments. They took the big pieces of furniture that belonged to our daughter and most of her belongings. My jaw dropped when I realized my helper had also packed her bags and simply said,

"Goodbye, madam, I am going with sir".

Later I discovered bank statements that indicated Michael had been paying the helper to spy on me by wiring her money directly to Sri Lanka. Irosha packed in such a hurry that she forgot about her notes left under her mattress and a copy of her new work contract. It became evident why she asked questions and kept a timetable of my whereabouts. Irosha and Michael also collaborated to switch her contract to his name, which allowed her to leave the family home. Michael had gone out of his way to orchestrate an evil plan, and I was the only one who had no idea about it. My heart sank to think that Mercedes was gone. My concern grew considerable when I thought about what would happen to her after her father returned to London. I sat in the reception to get a complete view of everyone taking my daughter's belongings. I didn't cry, I sat and watched. Gareth stood by the main door and avoided eye contact with me. I reminded him that his wife had just given birth to their daughter and here he was, helping Michael ruin my daughter's life. Gareth seemed not to care and kept looking into the distance, saying,

"I am just here to help."

The group of people who invaded the apartment left. Michael commented that he would keep a key since he was paying for the rent. A few days later, Michael's lawyers sent a message that he would come back with our daughter and the helper. Supposedly, to check what else our daughter wanted from the place. I am convinced his mistress guided him to do so. She holds a degree in manipulation and pain infliction. A friend named Zora agreed to be with me at the apartment when Michael showed up with our daughter. Zora wanted to ensure there were no dirty tricks. I was mainly in the kitchen but decided to go to the reception, trying to get a glance at my daughter. Mercedes saw me and casually said, "Hello". It was torture seeing my child in the flat and not being able to freely speak with her. The helper kept quiet and followed behind Michael and Mercedes. They packed and took whatever else they wanted and left. My friend and I also departed the building for a walk. It was then that I cried. The echo of the walls kept me company until I received the notice to vacate the apartment. I am so sorry, Mercedes, I failed you. I let you go with a monster who will only ruin your beautiful self because all he touches he eventually destroys.

On the other hand, I was bombarded by Camilla's request to gather documents. I spent hours thinking about it, not knowing where to start. She felt cross with me because she could not believe I had no online access to joint bank accounts. It was like a game of who could make me more nervous. Camilla was aware of Michael's over-controlling behavior. I knew the bank accounts existed because I had seen them in statements and tax documents but didn't have access or was allowed to perform movements or transactions. I realized that Camilla was heading on the wrong path or did not wish to listen to me, maybe because she saw me in such distress. But my mind has always remained sound, and I knew what she needed to know to make the right decisions.

Camilla requested the legal documents showing the company's constitution in Guatemala and sent them for translation to English. Hence, it was evident the property was legally an asset of the company, but she was relentless with her viewpoint. I became confused with the terminology Camila quoted about Italian property law. I think she had another case in which she was dealing with property in Italy and wanted to simplify my matter by resorting to what she was doing with the other case. With limited resources at my disposal, I hired a corporate lawyer in Guatemala to help her understand local corporate law and the rights of companies and shareholders. Regardless of my efforts to help, Ms. Fusco seemed to ignore the advice of an expert in Guatemalan corporate law. Without considering my sister's right as a shareholder, she went along with a property appraisal requested by the other party. Ignorant of legal proceedings, depressed, seeking temporary accommodation in England, and scared about my daughter staying in Hong Kong alone after finishing High School on Michael's request made me feel like I was sinking into quicksand.

Michael's legal team appointed me to be the one sourcing joint experts' property valuators. The other party said I spoke the language and was familiar with the country. I was then living in South Asia with limited resources and compromised health. Yet, no one seemed to acknowledge my circumstances, especially after I received their demands. First, I was not allowed to tell the possible valuator where the property was, the reason for the valuation, or the parties involved. The valuator had to follow The Royal Institute of British Architects (RIBA) standards, leaving possible candidates scratching their heads as the term was foreign to locals. You could imagine how difficult my task was—raising all kinds of red flags for corruption, extortion and money laundering. Second, Michael's solicitors insisted that it should be Michael choosing the joint expert. Neither Michael nor I could speak directly with the expert. Despite the specifics, Michael did contact the valuator asking her to "work" with him. Instead, the valuator wanted nothing to do with it; she understood the contract guidelines and called the lawyers complaining. When my legal team questioned his solicitors about the valuator's complaint, they seemed to have lied to protect Michael, stating that one of their solicitors had called with a question. Ridiculous statement, but by then, I got used to the outrageous claims of Michael's legal team. Never underestimate that greed is a dangerous foe.

Camilla seemed to be used to dealing with straightforward cases, and my case was nothing like it. Numerous times I explained Michael's character and his vengeful behavior.

"Be very careful, Camilla. Keep on your toes about Michael's every move", I said to her.

"He is unlike any other you may have met before, he is mean and will do anything in his power to win."

CHAPTER 9: THE LEGAL FIRMS

But she didn't believe me. I begged Camilla to freeze the $3 Million USD life insurance policy. I even traveled to New Jersey in the US to speak with the wealth manager who arranged the Mass Mutual policy. As far as he knew, they could freeze the account, but a court order was needed. I asked Camilla to act on my request, but she seemed to ignore the urgency of the matter.

Before the expert's report was due, a Guatemalan volcano named Fuego began spewing ashes. So, the joint valuator took the conservative step to hold to the report's release. Unfortunately, the volcano exploded on 3 June 2018. The volcano produced a dangerous ash column approximately 15 kilometers in height during the eruption. Pyroclastic flows, fast-moving clouds of hot gas and volcanic matter caused up to 2,900 people to perish during the destruction, according to local organizations. Many victims were never found. In addition, nearby towns were destroyed, and a golf club was submerged in lava.

The expert wrote an apology to the court for the delay and explained the situation. The property is only 16 kilometers away from the volcano. As expected, the evaluator recommended price adjustment due to the emergency and lack of confidence from future buyers. She was aware that her submission would take part in divorce proceedings and wanted the report to be realistic.

But despite the obvious, Michael was discontent with the expert's report. His strategy was to hide some of assets and make the company in Guatemala appealing to the court by finding an easy source of cash. Sadly, neither my solicitors nor the judges were as qualified as Michael in investments and money allocation. Michael's solicitors would give excuses to keep my solicitors waiting on loads of insufficiencies. Thus, making it easy for Michael to manipulate the court's perspective of our actual monetary situation. At the same time, he continued not to comply with disclosures. So, when the documents finally arrived, they would have lots of inexplicable money movements. Debts paid with his company's money, fake requirements from the Hong Kong government to hike his investment to $1 Million HKD, other deficits, over £30,000 GBP in an undisclosed pension plan and extra thousands to pay future taxes and newly open pension plans. There were all sorts of expenses, including £8,000 GBP for a ring, housing, travel costs, dentist bills, etc. The last three paid by his employer according to his work contract. I still wonder why an expert forensic accountant was not brought to oversee the complicated money movements in my divorce case. I was in distress seeing my solicitors so complaisant to Michael's moves. He kept dumping useless papers making my legal team waste time getting buried in nonsense instead of fulfilling insufficiencies. As a result, my legal bills grew and my case slowly derailed from justice.

Stewarts Law

Court proceedings in London were on their way as I was still in Hong Kong. One judge ordered Michael to pay for both legal fees and determine an amount for spousal maintenance. Finally, I could source a stronger solicitor

CHAPTER 9: THE LEGAL FIRMS

and be on the same footing for my legal representation. I proceeded to replace Camilla with Stewarts Law. I contacted one of their partners, who happened to be in Hong Kong on holiday. A few weeks later, Debbie took my case.

Along with Debbie came a senior associate, Nichola. The other party got notified, and my team began learning about my case. I also warned them about Michael's tactics. In the beginning, I felt secure. The solicitors' team appeared well-experienced. Michael began getting in arrears paying their bills, and rapidly, hundreds became thousands of pounds sterling. Michael's solicitors would constantly criticize Stewarts for how long they took to review my documents and their high fees. Payne Hicks Beach even dared to attack me in court for switching solicitors. Still, they conveniently forgot to mention that Michael had initially worked with Farrer & Co. I guess they were too honest, so Michael swappeCentury21

Michael had canceled the lease from the family home in Hong Kong, and I had to source a service apartment for the next two months until our daughter finished high school. I didn't want to leave her there alone. I wished for her to finish high school and head to England with me or the US with her brothers for a job internship in either country to ease her transition to her new home country. Michael was to pay for my new accommodation. I had given a deposit for the first month to secure the temporary place. To begin his attack, Michael canceled all our joint credit cards. I did not have the money to pay for the remaining rent during check-in. I scrambled to get the rest and moved to my studio. My friend Debra came to the flat, brought dinner, and we had a hot meal together. Debra, your visit on that day filled me with strength for the rest of the way until it was time to leave Hong Kong. Thank you again.

A plan was already prepared in my head for the relocation and removal from Hong Kong to London. After Michael decided we were moving to South Asia, he sent me there in a rush, and it took him three months before he caught up with our daughter and me; I was now getting expelled in a hurry. I was used to random locations and mentally prepared for the shipment and turmoil that accompanied removals. Michael had it on his work contract that his employee would pay for the relocation. I hired the same company we had used, AGS.

The day of the removal was approaching when I received an email from my solicitors. Michael wanted to be in the building during the removal. I wasn't sure why, as he had never helped with removals before. I wanted to be as far away from him as possible for safety reasons. My luck struck when the building issued an elevator service repair call. Our date for the move had to switch to accommodate the repair and the removal company. Michael was furious. After the belongings were packed and on the way to a container, he decided not to make the deposit or arrange payment for the shipment.

The removal company's manager contacted me, understandably upset and asking for a solution. I contacted Stewarts and asked for help. Instead of pressing for the agreed arrangement, I was asked to think of how to make the deposit. I was afraid of the removal company suing

CHAPTER 9: THE LEGAL FIRMS

me; every day costs them money to have a loaded container at the port without putting it at sea. I remember the only credit card in my name since 1993. The same one I gave to Michael when he had no credit and mine would allow him to buy his first new car. A-ha! I can use that, but who will reimburse me?

Nichola said, "Don't worry, we will make sure to mention it in court, Michael will get criticized and you will get the money to repay the card."

I should have never given my credit card. The money was never recovered, and Michael's behavior did not get reprehended in court. Until today, I got left with a debt of $16,000 USD plus huge interest, and only able to pay the interest payments on the debt.

Around April 2018, my daughter and I began to communicate again. She kept it a secret from her father. Mercedes and I would go out together for coffee, walks, shopping and gym. I loved listening to her tales, her contagious smile and seeing her eyes sparkle with enthusiasm. I can tell she felt regret for following her father's evil proposals but would not dare to cross him. It was deeply saddening to see her unfairly misguided, intimidated and scared by her own father.

The school year came to an end. To my surprise, Mercedes announced that she would remain in Hong Kong. Most of her school friends and boyfriend had left for the holidays or settled in a new country before university. Michael had planned to get his permanent Hong Kong residency but needed our daughter there to keep the show going. He never notified the local immigration authorities that he had relocated and was worked in London since September 2017. Instead, he would use the tactic of leaving with one passport and entering with his Hong Kong ID. Michael traveled to Hong Kong every month, telling his bosses in London he needed to check on his daughter. In reality, he "needed" to keep up his show or would have to start another seven-year term if the government found out he was working on another continent. I felt terrible for Mercedes and was disgusted that a narcissistic man could use and sacrifice his own daughter for his selfish purpose. I did notify the proper authorities, according to the investigator; when Michael got confronted, he denied it, and the immigration department decided not to perform a check. I am almost sure if Michael had been the one making the complaint, I would have been scrutinized.

It was time for me to relocate to London, particularly at the time when my legal matter was advancing in the Central Family Court of England. So, I departed Hong Kong terribly worried and brokenhearted as I left Mercedes behind. My story there began abruptly and ended the same way. I never had the chance to close that part of my life in Hong Kong. I still tremble with anxiety when I see pictures from my time there. One day, I will return and make my peace with the island.

My lodging arrangements in London were at a small Airbnb. I prepared for my first court appointment with boxes all over and two suitcases in the corner of the tiny place. It was almost summertime in London. I didn't want Michael to see me falling apart. So, for my first in-person court appointment, I dressed up in a pink dress, my curls

CHAPTER 9: THE LEGAL FIRMS

in a messy bun, high heels, and my signature look with long earrings.

My solicitor was not Debbie, a partner of the legal firm; I was told she was too expensive. My guess is Stewarts did not see the money poured as expected and decided to cut their bets short. With me in court was solicitor Nichola. Alongside her was barrister Nicholas Anderson. It was obvious Nick didn't bother reading into my case before the court hearing; his points were wrong and only made things worse by repeating a mistake Camilla Fusco had made in one of my initial forms. Unfortunately, his careless mistake helped raise doubts about the corrected content of the form during the final court hearing of December 2018. On the bench was Deputy District Judge Brenda Morris. She seemed to be in a bad mood and kept interrupting my barrister. Judge Morris took a glance at me with disdain. The wife should find a job and go to work, she said. My legal team and I were left perplexed by her quick solution to my matter. She most probably thought I was a woman who used to live from the money of others and took advantage of the poor husband who was making ends meet.[13]

When the court appointment ended, I asked my legal team, "What the hell happened in there? Is this what I will be facing in the Central Family Court?"

Nichola told me that it was a periodical meeting and that we would have more time to deal with all the issues in detail. My legal team also said that judges don't like women who look and dress well. They want to see suffering, sad eyes and somber victims. How disgusting, I thought. And now I had to play a game to please desensitized judges in court? The female population seems to keep following in the pool of playing rolls. While men dress well to impress judges, females must not.

My opinion differed a great deal from those of my solicitor. I insisted on the need to get every single chance to expose my husband's character. But my legal team's goal was almost of a factory mindset; deal with the divorce without significant complications, reach a settlement and move on to the next client. The physical and mental abuse were topics they didn't want to consider. I often hear from my solicitor the "no fault" term, but it is not as simple as that. There are ways to expose the wrongs of the other party. My mistake was trusting and accepting, consequently leaving a wolf dressed up like sheep among the flock. In 2022, an article read that finally, all divorces could be "no fault". [14] It stated that unhappy couples didn't have to fake evidence anymore to leave the marriage. I suppose the legal system was aware of the fraud going on. Why decide to turn a blind eye for 50 years instead of advocating for a new law to fulfill our present needs? Is it easy to live with corruption and crime rather than changing direction?

On the second Financial Dispute Resolution (FDR), Michael's barrister, Nicholas Wilkinson, complained to the court that the property's valuation was too low and applied for another valuation. Conveniently he forgot to mention who had chosen the property valuator, the recent volcanic eruption or their knowledge that the property was an asset to a foreign company. Looking in retrospect,

CHAPTER 9: THE LEGAL FIRMS

I am baffled at the fact that a property valuation was allowed in the first place.

In July 2018, Michael flew to Guatemala under false pretenses to check on the property, despite getting told that besides ashes, all was well. He made his way to the house around 6 p.m. and began banging and kicking the front door, demanding access. The following day, Michael contacted the corporate lawyer, asking her to draft a document so his forced entry would appear legal. The lawyer refused Michael's demands and called me and my sister Flory. He later showed up with three men and equipment to break the locks. In the meantime, with family members inside, the guardian and the house manager got terrorized by him with threats of imprisonment. I notified my solicitors in London. Michael's solicitors requested access to the property to get his independent property valuator. One of such "valuators" was Century21, the other a man an acquaintance of the owners of Century21. My family was furious with me for not doing anything about Michael's behavior. It was evident to them that my divorce was spilling Michael's poison over them. My elderly mother had to get transferred from the property in Antigua to the city to accommodate Michael's tantrum.

While Michael's late disclosures were coming, we were getting ready for another round in court. I began noticing discrepancies in Michael's pay slips. They were different from previous ones; the corporate font and color were not present. The numbers in his end-of-year tax document (P60) did not align; my signature had been falsified in the Hong Kong taxes for 2016/2017, and the list went on. I called my solicitor and was explicit about my findings. Their answer was that it was not to my best interest to get Michael in trouble because the judge would see him unfit to pay maintenance. And just like Camilla, they lost an opportunity to make wrong right.

I was becoming desperate and felt I had to do something about it. So, in August, I began thinking of a way to verify the documents. In my ignorance, I called human resources from Capula Investments. I asked to speak with someone regarding pay slips. I didn't ask for anyone specifically but got transferred to the head of the department. He was a soft-spoken gentleman. I identified myself; he, of course, knew about the divorce. He acknowledged that he understood my situation.

"I have divorced as well", he said. "I know how difficult it is, especially for our children."

He was not aware that I had already spoken to the wife of one of the partners in January 2018. I kept it to myself as it was not my intention to cause any harm. Sue knew about the physical abuse I suffered under Michael. When Sue learned about the stolen trade and the quality of person Michael was, she consulted her husband. I got put in touch with QC Alford. We spoke plenty during his Q&A sessions. In the end, Capula chose not to do anything about it, despite knowing the kind of risk Michael was posing for the company, and that was their fall.

I explained my concerns to the head of HR. I proposed sending him the documents in question to cross-check with the ones in Michael's file. But I was told that only a court order would allow him to do that. He referred me to a dedicated helpline for employees and their families and shared his direct phone number and email address. I thought that was the end of it. Until I heard from my solicitors. Apparently, Michael was called by HR and his boss. It is unknown to me what went on in the meeting. All I know is that Michael fabricated lies about my phone call. He told his solicitors that I had called with extortion and suicidal threats and would call the newspapers and make them accountable for it. Knowing Michael's mistress, a total low class, I could only target her for the ridiculous idea and choice of words. Michael's complaint gave his solicitors the perfect chance to win at all costs. My solicitors did not believe me and requested me to sign a document that I could have not signed if I knew what it meant. The paper was a notice for me to self-represent in court.

In mid-August 2018, Michael's legal team from Payne Hicks Beach appropriated the hearing set by my solicitors regarding a Maintenance Pending Suit (MPS), seeking unpaid legal fees order vs the husband. Ben Parry-Smith and Joshua Moger urged the court to take the appointment to issue a non-molestation order against me and expose my behavior. The only evidence was Michael's statement with a false narrative of what have taken place in a phone call. For the first time, I had to face court alone. Trembling with fear and without not knowing the protocol except for being respectful and telling the truth, I had no idea what else to do to defend myself.[15]

My son David provided his support and accompanied me to the court. While sitting in the waiting area,

Michael's solicitor, Ben-Parry Smith, approached me a few times with their barrister, Ben Wooldridge, from One Hare Court. They were coaxing me to sign a note, taking back any claim of abuse I could have ever made against Michael.

My message was simple, "Sirs, I am not going to lie for you."

But they returned again and told me that they knew the sitting judge was Deputy District Judge Morris. The same judge who sent me to work on my first court appearance. Michael's legal team was relentless with their bullying games. I got told that the judge didn't like me, and my lack of cooperation was wrong, thus aggravating my case. I was extremely nervous, and they were not helping. In the end, I agreed to keep the documents they wanted me to sign and knock on their waiting room before going into court. I never knocked. Minutes before the court session, the court's clerk served me with a non-molestation order. I was not surprised as I knew how Michael operates regarding intimidation techniques.

I entered the court, the judge was not District Judge Morris. The sitting judge was District Judge Gibbons; she was patient, kind and understanding of the fear I experienced by being self-representing. The other party began with hyperinflated and false statements to trash me. The judge asked me questions, and I replied politely with the truth. Unfortunately, Michael was about to surprise me once more. His solicitors proceeded to present a false sale contract. The "contract", on plain paper, with the old logo of Century21, without the broker's name and my signature falsified. Supposedly, I attempted to sell the property in 2017 for $3 Million USD. The franchise Century21 and Fine Homes in Antigua, Guatemala, is owned by two Canadian friends of Michael. Why did he wait so long to preset a "key" document? Why didn't Michael produce the valuations he claimed were done in July?

I questioned its validity and confirmed not seeing the document before. My credibility was getting tested, and the judge seemed confused with the valuation price and adjustment from the expert valuator. Michael's legal team did not have the courtesy to inform District Judge Gibbons about the adjustments made because of the volcanic eruption in Guatemala. The judge was also concerned about the "sale contract". District Judge Gibbons denied the non-molestation order. Instead, I signed an undertaking without finding facts or admission, as well as a court order prohibiting me from contacting or communicating with Michael's employer or future employers. Neither could I reach out to his business-related acquaintances, former or prospective clients, or anyone where I could damage his "reputation". And of course, the vast range of people included our friends. The judge's order left me with only a handful of people to rely on for help. Her Honor had no idea of the monster we were dealing with. Luckily, she ensured I got access to legal representation by issuing a "Pound per Pound" order and the right to investigate the Century21 "sale contract" document.

Michael decided not to keep up with payments to Stewarts Law. He claimed not to pay his legal fees. Per the Court Order, he should pay my legal team whatever he spent on his. Michael's dirty technique was evident. It was highly disappointing that Stewarts did not pursue Michael for their fees. Their mistake cost me plenty of headaches, and not exposing Michael's fraud would cost me my case.

I once heard that your lawyers are only as good as you are. Such was proven correct in my case. I had no knowledge of the law and was not in the corporate workforce for years, making me live in a false reality. I was not connected, nor did I know how to find the right advice, so I believed, like a dying patient believes in their doctors. No one knows your story and circumstances better than you. When your legal representation is not dedicated to 100% of your interest and ignores you; run, run for your life, because your problems are about to get worse. Until eventually, karma slowly but surely puts things right.

Vardags

In September 2018, while I was desperately trying to source legal representation, a friend stumbled on an article from *The Sunday Times*. It read:

> "Vardags law firm has announced the launch of an exclusive £10 million loan fund provided by Schneider Financial Solutions Ltd to help fund complex divorce cases. The Access to Justice Loan Fund will be available for people whose spouses are trying to stop them from getting their fair share in divorce cases and those trapped in unhappy marriages which they cannot

afford to escape. The Access to Justice Loan Fund is about bringing to justice people who seek to deprive their wife or husband of money by hiding it, not declaring it, giving it to family members, putting it offshore, squirrelling it away in complex trusts or businesses, and deliberately delaying and complicating divorce proceedings," says Vardags. "This loan fund will allow the financially weaker spouse to fight this contemptible behavior and hopefully deter others from engaging in this dishonest activity in the courts."[16]

It was the answer I had been waiting for. I googled Vardags and contacted their divorce department. I was asked to complete the usual form to crosscheck the conflict of interest. After a phone call with Maria Fiorito, I was appointed to meet with solicitor Terrence Trainor.[17]

Terrence and Maria seemed patient, caring and understanding. Maria was working on getting certified as a European Lawyer. Terrence had recently relocated from Australia to work with Vardags in London. We talked about how I had found the legal firm, and then Terrence asked me how I was planning to fund the litigation. I mentioned the "Pound per Pound" order from District Judge Gibbons. We spoke about my case and previous incidents. Terrence wanted to accept my legal matter but needed a deposit. I mentioned having only £5000 GBP from spousal maintenance, but it was mostly to pay rent. He left the room for a few minutes. On his return, I was told that Vardags had agreed to take my divorce matter. But I had to leave several thousand in deposit. I feel that as individuals, Terrence and Maria had the best intentions for my case. I warned them about Michael, but Terrence and Maria did not listen either. I began feeling trapped, as if in an eternal déjà vu. Michael used the same tactic of delaying payments; my legal cost was not getting met. At one point, his legal team argued that if their client was not paying them, he could not pay my legal team either.

Not sure why Vardags was too slow and did not file a pending maintenance suit to secure the funds to cover their cost. There was one already set but postponed by Stewarts Law because the regular court appointment date came too close for both hearings to take place. Time was flying; our court appointment in the Central Family Court (CFC) was towards the end of October. Stewarts kept my file due to the money owed. Terrence received all the documents I had, including email correspondence between Michael, Camilla, the legal team of Stewarts and me, and those related to the false sale contract from Century21.

Terrence told me before the court hearing that the barrister he wanted was unavailable in my case. But he had received recommendations of a junior. So, we set a meeting to meet with Jamie. My opinion is that Vardags did not see a hefty sum in my client's account and decided to limit the expenses on my case. Vardags had resources within, including a team for criminal investigations, but only for the big money spenders. And The Access to Justice Loan Fund was nowhere to be found. It was my obligation to point out to my legal representative the type of character Michael was and provide in detail the crimes he had committed.

During my first court appointment with Vardags, Jamie had the opportunity to mention that the Century21 was fraudulent, that we had permission to investigate it and that we would proceed to do so. Although the other party objected, we raised the issue of Michael still having many insufficiencies not satisfied since he was ordered to comply in August. Information about the accounting and shares from his friend in Hong Kong AMP Credit Technology and Gojoko. He stated that he was not allowed to access the company's financials, those being privileged documents. Still, Jamie argued that Michael was on the board of directors and a shareholder, granting him access to the information.

Michael's solicitors sent a batch of the documents to fulfil some of the pending deficiencies a day before the November pre-hearing court appointment. Before the hearing, my legal team and I checked the submitted papers in the court's waiting area. I noticed a 2017/2018 Hong Kong tax document that had the wrong year inputted. It was not the same form Michael had presented to the Hong Kong authorities. We also had evidence that Michael falsified my signature on the previous Hong Kong tax submission; I was confident he had done the same for 2017/2018. So, he used a generic form and gave us that. Remember, Michael didn't want the Hong Kong government to know he had left in September 2017. Neither was he keen to raise any suspicions about the family, marriage status, living arrangements and our change of address.

Hence continuing to put the address we no longer had at 41 C Stubbs Road, Mid-Levels East when filing governmental forms. Michael's legal address continues to be a sham in documents where he appears as a shareholder and board of directors and company registrars until today.

I asked my barrister and my solicitor to confront Michael about the discrepancy. Jamie asked to speak with Michael's legal team. Nicholas Wilkinson was the barrister for the other party; Ben Parry-Smith and Joshua Moger the solicitors. The reply Jamie received was that Michael could not answer at the moment because he had a headache and couldn't concentrate on our question. So, the question was never answered, and we never got the original copy of the actual Hong Kong taxes from 2017/2018.

As I mentioned before, Capula's legal advisor QC Alford from Latham & Watkins, and I have been in contact since January 2018. Around mid-October, Barrister Andrea Monk from the same legal firm called in an intimidating manner asking me not to attempt to contact their legal firm. Sue, the wife of one of Capula's partners, already knew of the physical abuse I suffered under Michael and the financial investment trade from Symmetry Investment. My points had gone across months ago, so what had changed? Were they afraid I would mention Sue, so they decided to throw me under the bus? Knowing Michael's character, they had chosen not to investigate. Capula Investment ignored that Michael was a physical, mental and economic abuser. I am unsure what Michael told Capula's legal team or what type of falsehood he presented. But I can confirm that I never signed a "retraction document"

CHAPTER 9: THE LEGAL FIRMS

that Michael so badly wanted me to sign and the pictures of physical abuse are from June not September.

My legal team and I were preparing a conduct statement against Michael, and their call weakened my argument. I kept making the same mistake about trusting people and believing we were seeking truth and justice; foolish me, it was apparent that greed covered more ground than good intentions. 6 November was the date of the pretrial hearing. We began working with my legal team about Michael's conduct statement. On 10 November, an expert from Key Forensic began investigating the suspected fraudulent Century21 sale contract. On 19 November, we had the Allegations of Fraud Statement ready to file. Other evidence included my claims of falsification of my signature on IRS consent, tax documents, bank and financial accounts reports. Finally, on 22 November, the statement was file.

Chapter 10

Fraud, Perjury and Mockery

We were getting closer to the final hearing set for 10 December. My solicitors were nervous. There were no funds, and Michael continued to ignore making payments; we were all on edge. Usually paid in advance, Jamie decided to give us credit to get to the final hearing.[18]

The final court hearing arrived. Ben Parry-Smith and Joshua Moger were the solicitors, and Nicholas Wilkinson was the barrister for Michael's side. My legal team was barrister Jamie, and solicitors Maria Fiorito and Terrence Trainor. The other party were determined to portray me as a liar, jealous and deranged woman. So, when it was my turn to speak, I faced Michael and told the judge I was on antidepressants due to my husband. He had created a mess in our family, and our children were suffering because of him.

Nicholas Wilkinson opened with what they called discrepancies in the property valuation in Guatemala. He insisted I had tried to cover up the true value of the property. Their evidence was two further appraisals performed by Michael's independent evaluators, a friend from Century21 and a second one from a man who usually works with Century21. Let me remind you that the appraisals took place in July 2018, but never before had Michael disclosed the result of such estimates until the final hearing.

The judge seemed confused when the barrister for the other party stated that the husband was seeking to get the property sold in a foreign country.

"So, Mr. Wilkinson", the judge said, "Do you want me to tamper with an asset of a company?"

"Your honor, you see, the company is not a real company. Mrs. Hieb made it look like it, but she is the majority shareholder, and her sibling has the rest of the shares."

The Guatemalan lawyer presented vast information to Vardags and explained it via phone conferences. But the court did not want to hear about Guatemalan law. Vardags did not demonstrate much of what the Guatemalan lawyers urged him to do. District Judge Mulkis denied any legal guidance or documents from the Guatemalan corporate lawyer because he seemed to follow the lead of PHB and Nicholas Wilkinson. The latter of which did not seem to be one bit knowledgeable about Guatemalan law. The Judge and Michael's legal team claimed that the documents provided by the corporate lawyer were only to aid my case. Michael's legal team was relentless in repeating a lie as if the more times they said it would make it accurate.

CHAPTER 10: FRAUD, PERJURY AND MOCKERY

Any company's compositions and law structure in Guatemala are readily available on the internet. Proving many times before how "resourceful" they were, Michael's legal team seemed to keep ignoring what did not suit their agenda instead of following the law. Still, they choose to accept what their client fed them because such is defensible in court—the right to believe whatever their client tells them. Were they also afraid of Michael's tantrums or power-hungry nature?

At one point District Judge Mulkis got cross with Nicholas Wilkinson for insisting the company was not a company. The Judge asked Wilkinson if he attempted to turn a circle into a square.

Nicholas Wilkinson replied, "Yes, your honor. I will prove it is possible."

"That I want to see", said the judge.

My legal team objected and complained that Michael was attempting to portray the wrong picture of the circumstances. They also exposed the unwillingness of the husband to fulfil by overdue insufficiencies and other pending documents he needed to disclose.

Terrence, my leading solicitor insisted that my sister, the other shareholder to state her point in court regarding my mother's and her living arrangements in the Guatemalan property. My sister was right; if she had nothing to do with my divorce, why should she get involved? But Terrence pressed, and she reluctantly acceded.

I had no idea that following Terrence's advice would eventually lead to my family getting harmed and ultimately breaking it apart. On the court day designated for my sister (also a shareholder of the Guatemalan company) to speak via phone, the court ran out of time, meaning she wasted her day waiting. Annoyed by the inconvenience and thinking twice about the costly international call, she warily agreed to call the next day. I don't remember what time of the day it was when she finally received the green light to ring the court. She had just finished doing business with a government office in a nearby town after taking mom to a medical exam. Once on the phone, Michael's legal team yielded a brutal attack against my sister.

Rather than asking questions regarding the agreed topic of living arrangements, barrister Nicholas Wilkinson tangled the questions to confuse my sister and cross-examined her on other legal matters without her lawyer being present. The quality of the audio and having a translator did not help. The audacity of Michael's legal team to mock my sister, insisting on her exact location. She provided the town's name; Michael, Ben Parry-Smith and Joshua Moger jumped like hyenas to check on Google Maps. Nicholas Wilkinson called my sister a liar and told the judge that if she was running errands in a governmental office far from the property, it was because she did not live in Antigua. Michael's legal team also questioned our mom's medical appointment, as if it was not customary to go for medical exams in other hospitals that may have the equipment that her nearby clinic didn't.

The cherry on top was raising suspicion by asking which primary school my sister's son was attending. She said none and elaborated that he studied in the city. To

CHAPTER 10: FRAUD, PERJURY AND MOCKERY

avoid confusion during translation, I asked Jamie my barrister to confirm to the court that her son was in his twenties and attending university in Guatemala City. Michael's legal team jumped from their seats with the absurd request to produce evidence of Marlon's age. Even though phones are not allowed in court, somehow, I was permitted to send my sister a text requesting her cooperation. Flory did not want to share anything about her one and only son. So, I begged, and a few minutes later, she sent a screenshot of Marlon's birth certificate. Flory also sent a picture with Marlon smiling.

Needless to say, how frustrated my sister was with Terrence and me for putting her in a ring with bullies and being unable to defend herself. After court, I called Flory to thank her. In a solemn tone, she asked me to ensure that nothing wrong would happen to her son or the document. By then, my family was aware of the illicit actions of Michael's lawyers in Guatemala and knew how dangerous that bunch was. I had no idea that my failure attempts to keep the promise I made to my sister about preserving my nephew's safety would bring unimaginable harassment and intimidation.

A day early, the phone call with the housekeeper Ms. Nilda de Leon was another fiasco. For starters, she was expecting a call from the court. But instead, it was up to the housekeeper to make the phone call to England. I could not believe Terrence did not communicate such an essential detail, mainly because he had pushed for Nilda to get called as a witness. I knew the property she tended to didn't have an international calling service. My family had to lend her money to buy time at a nearby calling center. The person in charge of the small calling service allowed a few minutes at a time. The housekeeper kept getting distracted by the men pointing out that the time was about to expire. Michael's legal team asked her where my elderly mother was.

Perplexed about the question, Nilda replied, "At the house."

My barrister explained the situation to the judge, who seemed skeptical. The entanglement of questions led to a very long and ultra-expensive call, to the point of the phone booth cutting the call altogether. Nicholas Wilkinson jumped, telling the judge the housekeeper disconnected because she was lying, didn't want to answer more questions and accused her of not cooperating. Within minutes, Nilda called back and did her best to explain. Picture a humble woman, terrified of Michael and now terrorized by Nicholas Wilkinson and the judge. In January 2019, Michael's legal team will twist this incident and mislead the court.

The Big Lie

Imagine the security check when you enter a government building; such is the process in the Central Family Court. All visitors need to pass through a security checkpoint. Michael and his two solicitors were ahead. They did not take note of me, and I didn't have much in my hands, so I passed the screening quickly. In the hallway, Michael was laughing, the trio speaking.

CHAPTER 10: FRAUD, PERJURY AND MOCKERY

While tapping on his briefcase, I overheard Michael saying, "This will be the deadly blow because I need to win this."

The solicitors laughed, and one asked, "Really?"

Ben Parry-Smith said, "By all means, give me what you have."

Knowing Michael, I quivered with his words, and instead of heading toward the elevator, I diverted to the bathroom. I drank cold water, waited a few minutes, and then headed towards the elevator leading me to the designated courtroom.

The court hearing began, and Michael's barrister stated an urgent matter that the court needed to be aware of. He presented a copy of a simple email, about four lines in length. Supposedly from Michael's boss. It read:

> "12 December 2018, I hereby confirm that we have informed you of the decision to terminate your employment as Chief Risk Officer at Capula. We have asked you to cooperate in the transition as we search for a replacement in the coming months. As discussed, this decision is not in any way related to your performance as CRO, nor have we found any evidence to question your fitness and propriety. The decision is due to the Board of Partner's general concern for ongoing reputation risk stemming from your personal life. Sincerely, Fred."

I thought, who in their right mind terminates their Chief Risk Officer by email, stating that it's due to his personal life? Jamie, my barrister and my solicitors, exchanged a few words. When Jamie addressed the judge, he showed his disbelief at how the other party didn't seem distressed regarding the terrible news he had just received. He argued that we needed a person from Capula to approach the court by any possible medium to answer a few questions. The other side objected, stating the wife had already caused enough damage to their client. Asking Capula to get further involved would embarrass them and jeopardize Michael's further agreements with the company. The judge seemed to agree with Michael's legal team, and we in exchange were denied any possibility of calling Michael's bluff.

My legal team brought forward the Century21 fraudulent sale contract. I produced evidence with every travel stamp from my previous and current passport. I was not in Guatemala during any of the dates given by Michael. He instantly changed his story by claiming the year was not 2017 but rather 2014. Michael seemed to have the judge's sympathy. And he was not letting the luxury of manipulation go to waste. Unfortunately, the judge overlooked essential contractual requirements, such as lacking the broker's name. Which property broker would arrange a contract expecting 3% to 6% of $3 million USD and not put their name?

District Judge Mulkis seemed not to be troubled by Michael changing the year from 2017 to 2014. In his second attempt Michael claimed I had completed the form. Unfortunately for him, I was able to prove his peculiar handwriting and the way he wrote numbers. Michael seemed to have more jokes in his bag. He later argued that the issue was confusing and suddenly, remembered me asking for him to complete the form, and I had signed.

District Judge Mulkis accepted Michael's abrupt change on narrative and ignored the forensic expert report which regarded the Century21 sale contract as fraud and containing my signature falsified. The judge also ignored my statement of physical abuse and the evidence submitted. The judge declared that he continued to believe I had signed the Century21 "sale contract". The words of District Judge Mulkis paralyzed me. I cried in disbelief, but my crying only made Michael smile with pleasure.

The following question lingered in my head for a very long time. How could the judge agree with Michael's claims on the sale contract dating from 2014 but deny a necessary inquest on $4.575 million USD from selling a townhouse we owned in New York City, leaving a Net amount of $2,320,277.65 USD. The answer is upholding, and called "discretionary power", a potent power entrusted to ALL judges. Such could make or destroy lives. It is not earned by merit nor by peer or senior reviews. It is a mere way to help judges expedite legal matters because the court lacks judges.

In November 2018, my team went after Michael's 2014 US tax filings. It was vital to perform a forensic track of the money and uncover any hidden assets Michael may have. To our surprise, District Judge Mulkis denied access to the tax records. He ratified that it was only fair to backtrack two years since the initiation of divorce proceedings. Michael got questioned about the money from the property sale. He replied that we paid the remaining mortgage, taxes, fees leaving a Net of $1.1 million USD which we had already spent. Evidence? None. The judge seemed satisfied with the reply, so we had to accept the ridiculous answer.

On the third day in court, Michael's legal team argued that I held power of attorney over the other shareholder's shares. I was astounded by the ease at which Michael was feeding falsehood to the court. Emails he suddenly found in a server he built and ran from home were the ingenious and ONLY evidence. The one-page email contained four messages from 2013 showing different type settings, some significantly larger as if randomly inserted. Still, the remittance of the lawyer remained the same size as in the presumably first message. The email Michael claimed I sent to the lawyer replied with a different email address than the one addressed to the lawyer. The discrepancies on the date showed first the year, then month and lastly the day: 2013-01-09. If the person inserting numbers tried making it look credible and wanted to show Greenwich Mean Time (GMT), they should have entered 22:47 as Guatemala is five hours behind the said time. Is the fraudster so ignorant that copied part of the date stamp from the lawyer's "first" message without knowing what GMT means? Michael's barrister, Nicholas Wilkinson, seemed proud to present yet another last-minute surprise. Why didn't Wilkinson ask my sister about the "power of attorney" when they crossed examined her? My legal team looked at me with discontent.

CHAPTER 10: FRAUD, PERJURY AND MOCKERY

I immediately responded, "Not possible. Michael is wrong!"

I am not sure how District Judge Mulkis accepted such a grave accusation, especially at the very last minute of the final court hearing and without having at least a copy of the said power of attorney to support their claim. I got left with no time to repute and prove the falsehood of Michael's accusation.

The other party continued with their attempts to raise suspicion. Remember, their target was jeopardizing my credibility. I remember the eyes of the judge on me; it was intimidating. I wanted to scream, but my legal team had made it clear about not demonstrating my feelings in court. I looked at my team, and instead of finding support, I noticed they were upset. When the court hearing ended, I asked my solicitors to speak with their fraud and computer expert department. I don't think they did because I found the abovementioned discrepancies a year later. What was Vardags thinking? A small amount of money could have squashed Michael's fraudulent emails. I cannot avoid feeling discontent with how my solicitors handled my legal matter.

The following year during appeal, I proved that I had been a victim of Michael's wicked slander. It took a great deal of work and money to solve the mystery of Michael's false claims. The findings jolted me. His lawyer in Guatemala, Oscar Estuardo Paiz Lemus, had somehow gained access to voided documents from governmental archives from 2013-2014. It was then when all made sense. During medical treatment, my sister, a second shareholder, independently opted for a power of attorney to benefit me in an emergency. Such power of attorney had expired in 2014, months after being drafted. I realized why the other party never provided a copy to District Judge Mulkis. They knew the Power of Attorney had elapsed long ago.

We were approaching the final day of court appointments in December 2018. In a strange request, Michael's solicitors asked the judge to excuse their client for being late; he was getting a yearly review by his boss. When Michael arrived, he flagged a paper, passed it to his solicitors and then to his barrister, Nicholas Wilkinson, he shared it with the judge. My team and I were the last to read it. It was Michael's year-end review, which more or less stated that he had done well during the year but needed to work on his temper and how he managed his team. Nicholas Wilkinson got carried away with his criticism stating the husband was a good employee, he had worked hard during the year. And because of me, he had been dismissed and was now unemployed. I know how Michael reacts to getting terminated from work, and trust me, he is not joking and smiling as he did two days before. Besides, it's illogical to get dismissed from work, then reviewed and praised by the same person who recently showed you the door. Knowing Michael, he would have sued Capula Investments in the blink of an eye. But unfortunately, the judge seemed very one-sided and accepted whatever trash Michael and his legal team presented in court.

During the last days of the final court hearing, finally, Michael handed over the financial statements of his startup company, Bahlam Core Ltd., AMP Credit

CHAPTER 10: FRAUD, PERJURY AND MOCKERY

Technology in Hong Kong and Gojoko in London. The companies in Hong Kong didn't have the proper hallmark required by law, the accountant and auditor(s) name and signature. The financial reports contained pages seemingly from an old tax version and one or two new pages inserted without being assembled in a proper numerical or logical sequence. My barrister argued that Michael had taken until the very last moment to hand over the financials, and we had no time to verify them. But the judge commented that the husband had fulfilled pending deficiencies. My legal team were previously briefed on Michael's involvement when linking Gojoko and AMP Credit Technologies. He was to profit from helping Gojoko and their sister company My Community Bank, using AMP lending system program already created rather than making a new one from scratch. The judge asked Michael if the two said companies were linked, and Michael denied it. My claims, proving the opposite, were not evaluated or cross checked with my evidence. I was furious as we had evidence but Terrence kept telling me that the judge had already asked Michael. He had denied it and we could not challenge the argument.

Some of pages inserted had summarized financial losses in all three companies. Without proper evidence, Michael claimed to lose 90% of the value of his investment in Gojoko and AMP Credit Technologies. The judge accepted the losses, as well as extensive borrowing over his startup financial consulting company Bahlam Core Ltd., and from his life insurance policy leaving his visible assets at a low cash value. Michael deserves an

Emmy Award for his acting in court and keeping a straight face.

The time came to cross-examine the joint valuator about her appraisal. It was strange that suddenly the usual translator was not available for days to come. My solicitors began scrambling for a replacement but couldn't source one in a hurry. Interestingly enough, Payne Hicks Beach offered one. After a break, the judge was upset because we had taken long sourcing an interpreter. The other side looked like champions for having saved the day. When the translator began, the lack of her ability as a translator became apparent. It was horrific witnessing this woman speaking nonsense. She couldn't or didn't want to translate. I confirmed with Maria what I was observing and urged for Terrence and Jamie's attention, telling them what Maria and I were hearing. Then, in desperate attempts for the judge to listen to my comments, I became louder as I called the translator many mistakes.

"She's not translating! That is not what the joint expert is saying!"

Maria's primary language is Italian but, she is also proficient in Spanish. I told Maria that the so-called translator was not doing an honest job.

"What's going on? Maria, please ask Terrence to mention it to the judge!"
Instead, of listening to my pleas Terrence asked me to remain quiet.

"The translator is a professional; if you keep at it, the judge will expel you from the court", Terrence said.

CHAPTER 10: FRAUD, PERJURY AND MOCKERY

I felt as if speaking to a brick wall. The judge looked at me and asked the valuator a couple of questions. The evaluator couldn't understand because the translation was wrong. Then, District Judge Mulkis asked the joint valuator,

"Did you see any clothes? Were there any clothes hanging in the closet?"

The valuator replied, not remembering that detail. As if valuators are supposed to check closets for personal items. So, her reply helped the other party to push the assumption that no people were living at the property. The miss information continued; Michael fabricated that the property's antiqueness was two hundred years to help support his proposed "value". His two independent valuators have gone as far as to claim that it was over two-hundred-fifty years old. But the joint valuator provided a conservative estimate of ninety-six years when asked in a questionnaire.

As per the helper and gardener, the joint valuator inquired about two original adobe walls in the house. Although they have undergone renovation, the thickness led her to make an educated guess. She also knew that once, the house was part of the adjacent property, now a primary school. So, the walls had to be around the same period. However, she never put the estimated antiquity of the property in her appraisal because it was not part of her job.

During the final court hearing in December, the joint valuator again received the question about the property's antiquity. She expresses a more conservative opinion by dating it between fifty and sixty years. The other party's trivial questions helped to discredit my legal team, the joint expert, and me further. In my opinion, she had done an honest job. She studied comparable prices and valued the property at $1.5 Million USD. Before submitting her appraisal, the volcano erupted, and she explained her modifications to the two legal teams. In her final assessment, the join expert also included an optimistic $1.350 Million USD and a pessimistic sell price of $1.2 Million USD. I could not immediately contradict Michael's narrative. Eventually, I sourced the right person to perform due diligence and found evidence to prove Michael and his team's false statements. The official government Property Registrar's Bureau demonstrated that in 2018, the property was only 70 years old.

I knew my team was acting less than efficiently. For me, it was a nightmare attending court. We were getting crushed unfairly by the other party. Ben Parry-Smith gave us his flagrant self. He would bully Terrence, my principal solicitor in the court's hallways, not caring if I was present or not. Perry-Smith would launch accusations out of place.

"Stop Mrs. Hieb's uncooperative behavior. Control your client, your behavior is unacceptable, and I will report you to the Solicitors Regulator Authority if you don't cooperate."

I asked Terrence why would he allowed Ben Parry-Smith to treat him with such disrespect? Terrence was polite, possessed a calm demeanor, and told me he refused to engage in unproductive behavior. Nicholas Wilkinson did his part; I could feel his hatred. He could have used a more

CHAPTER 10: FRAUD, PERJURY AND MOCKERY

human approach. Still, Wilkinson seemed to enjoy being a bully. The way he pleasantly trashed me and made sure the judge remember that I was a minority and foreigner. I often heard, "People like Mrs. Hieb." I detest his false appearance of politeness.

In his last attempts to derail the process, Michael resourced to his dubious lawyers in Guatemala. Yes, dubious! I say this with remarked tone because Oscar Estuardo Paiz Lemus and the very Michael Hieb have been under criminal investigation in Guatemala since 2019 for fraud including altering legal documents. He had done it in England and thought he would get away in Guatemala too.

On 13 December 2018, Oscar Estuardo Paiz Lemus lent himself to prepare a document with falsehood which found its way to the mere desk of District Judge Mulkis, and was submitted after the time limit for evidence had elapsed. Judges are hard to locate within courts, let alone, magically passing documents directly and after the fact.

The "testimony" lacked the necessary legal seals to make it valid. It was dated 5 October 2018. No reason was given for the two women to confirm their names, national ID number and the motivation to issue the document. Yeni and Flory denied taking part in such a statement. They also confirmed that they had never met Oscar Esturado Paiz Lemuz. A separate exhibit shows Yeni as the owner of the apartment. My sister Flory appeared as co-owner because she had cosigned the mortgage so Yeni could acquire the apartment. The document is from 2010; a page showing the record voided is omitted.

Interestingly, Paiz Lemus did not perform his search in the registrar until 9 December 2018, accordingly to the same document he presented as evidence. How could he justify the document issued by Flory and Yeni on 5 October same year? Neither Michael nor my solicitor asked him that question. Unfortunately, I was unable to access Guatemalan government sites from England. Lawyers in Guatemala check records for the said document after the Christmas holiday season. My sister's lawyer identified the attached as no longer valid. Once again, Paiz Lemus had attempted to mislead the Judge. It is alarming how Paiz Lemus misused personal and private information and the identification numbers of Yeni and Flory for self-serving and illicit purposes. Michael was very aware of my family's happenings in Guatemala, especially Flory's, because he was close to her and in constant communication due to the property renovation. If she was buying a property, I am sure she would have asked for us to provide advice. Michael knew the document was untrue but accepted it and introduced it to the Central Family Court in England.

Jamie, my barrister, was in disbelief about Michael's legal team's audacity and lack of ethics. Vardags threatened Payne Hicks Beach with a complaint to the Solicitor Regulator Authority, I pushed for it to take place but they never filed it. Maybe Vardags didn't want enemies and I was just a client. I got briefed on a draft email prepared by Jamie for the judge. Quickly did I learn that judges don't like complainers. There was a delicate line between requesting the judge's time and steering him into the "rules of law" which barristers are trained to do. Jamie urged the

CHAPTER 10: FRAUD, PERJURY AND MOCKERY

judge not to read the document. He also mentioned how the foreign company's lawyer urged the court to received crucial information regarding the binding law in Guatemala. But the judge had refused because he considered it late. Yes, the evidence from the corporate lawyer was one day late because no expert in Guatemala would have ever imagined a judge would willingly steer a citizen to commit fraud, reinforcing the endorsement of property not legally owned. District Judge Mulkis replied he would not read the note sent by Paiz Lemus. Remember that curiosity killed the cat because the subsequent steps taken by the judge aggravated the legal matter.

The divorce hearing ended. I was in limbo. How could my solicitors allow such a deception? Ringing in my ears are my pleads to Terrence,

"Do something! The judge is getting misled."

I would fume inside to see Terrence cowering over the dishonest conduct of my husband.

On December 19, just a few days after the final court hearing, District Judge Mulkis handed over his ruling. It must have been impressive witnessing the speed at which he read the massive pile of about 13 court bundles prepared by both parties. According to the judge, the house in Guatemala was too beautiful to turn into a warehouse to distribute my coffee and too big for me to live. And that the volcanic eruption was not severe enough to diminish the property's value. Amazed by the Judges' lack of respect for the victims, I felt as if he was not in touch with reality and the magnitude of the tragedy.

The judgement focused on the foreign property; Guatemalan law binding the company and its shareholders' rights were ignored. The property was to get sold. From the sale proceeds, 50% for Michael and 50% for me after tax fees and legal bills. The latter undermining the fact that Michael had been paying his legal team with our money while starving mine. But first Michael had to sell the property. Also, I had to comply with a list of ridiculous Unless Orders set by District Judge Mulkis in one of his several changes to his "Final Judgement". Some of the items included providing Michael with a certified copy of my sister's Guatemalan passport, National Identification card and copy of the Power of Attorney, which did not exist, all keys to the property in Guatemala, and changing the property's phone account to Michael's name (which in Guatemala is impossible without documents identifying the legal person appointed) as old phone lines belong to the property owner(s). But at this point, Guatemalan law or its requirements were dishonored. The Guatemalan lawyers questioned what type of law was practiced in England because it seemed worse than the established in third-world countries. More of the unless orders required me to write and sign an irrevocable authorization to the security surveying company stating Michael was the sole legal and beneficial owner of the company and that he had the exclusive rights to occupying the property.

Regarding corporate bank accounts, I was to provide Michael with a complete list of accounts and executed deeds giving him sole signatory power over them. The cruelest one was that neither my mother, sister, nor I could inhabit the property any longer, leaving three people displaced. Four years later and Michael has not sold the property. Was it because his price is ridiculous or because the fraud he committed is tying the property into the criminal courts? Tell us, Michael, which is it?

Regarding Michael's extravagant life insurance policy/saving and investing vehicle. He claimed having borrowed extensively against it, leaving it with a low value of $4,258.50 USD. I claimed it was worth at least the yearly premium of $108,143.49 USD, which he had recently claimed. Without evidence of the actual value, District Judge Mulkis agreed to the "current value" given by Michael and ordered the amount split in half between Michael and me. Our joint bank accounts containing a few thousand were to get split in half between us. In one of his orders, District Judge Mulkis imposed on me to get a decree absolute by mid-January 2019, just weeks after the final court hearing. Such action immediately left me without certain privileges as wife, and medical insurance to cover my needed medical procedure, known to both sets of solicitors since the beginning of divorce proceedings. Unfortunately, I didn't have the luxury of taking time off and getting the surgery due to the turbulent situation. I hoped to end the legal matter and get medical treatment, but that never happened.

The judged issued a worldwide freezing order injunction as urged by the other party. Michael legal team claimed that I may sell the property while he was drafting his judgement. Michael and I were to keep our own company in Hong Kong. My company was worth $5,000

USD, whereas Michael's was $100,000 USD. So I insisted on the value of each company to get registered in the judgement. But the other party argued that it was unnecessary, and the judge agreed.

Judge Mulkis seemed convinced that it was my fault that Michael lost his job because I called Capula back in August 2018. But, if Capula wanted to dismiss Michael because of my call, they would have done it then. The court did not consider Michaels' ability to lose his job because of his temper and character. So far, he has changed employment three times from 2019 to 2022. The Judge's reaction to the fake event of Michael losing his job was capping spousal maintenance to a maximum of five years for a quarter of a century marriage. From 1 January 2019 until 2021, a meagre amount, not enough to pay rent, utilities and immediate needs. I would receive only half of the original amount after two years. In February 2019, the judge changed his final order to grant spousal maintenance only after all his Unless Orders fully complied, a task impossible to fulfil. Michael was not going to leave an opportunity to see me struggling go to waste, so, for two years he claimed to not be working. Consequently, I expected to survive from air particles.

District Judge Mulkis denied me any money from Michael's bonus or compensation from his termination package from Capula. Imagine the relief Michael felt when he did not have to share funds from a settlement he would not have. In addition, the judge stated that I should not receive spousal maintenance if Michael remained unemployed. But justice is sweet and caught up with Michael

CHAPTER 10: FRAUD, PERJURY AND MOCKERY

as he did lose his job in January 2019. The liar immediately ran to complain to our friends about getting sacked from work because of me. How stupid was Michael to think my buddies would not tell me that he had confirmed his dismissal date? District Judge Mulkis was clear about me not getting permission to apply for further espousal maintenance.

My solicitors in London washed their hands of me, stating they were not familiar with Guatemalan law. Still, when they requested the advice from a senior lawyer in Guatemala, they received plenty of it. If they chose to ignore it is a separate issue. The miscarriage of law carried in The Central Family Court of England left a massive fraud issue in Guatemala.

Imagine a position where you can either face prison in England or prison for fraud in Guatemala. It was not only about assigning documents and shares to Michael, the main issue was handing over total control to such a person.

Inhumane orders included not receiving spousal maintenance until I executed the shared transfer order and fully complied with all unless orders. To me, such abuse is blackmail. The court was forcing me into a dangerous position leaving me unable to defend myself against fraud in Guatemala.

Unless all the requests complied and the sale of the property took place, Michael was not liable for sharing half of the money held in pension funds which comprised an amount of £78,600 GBP and distribution of other money including maintenance. After the property's sale,

Michael would pay me for the pension funds from his proceeds, leaving his pockets intact.

The court designated Michael to sell the property and market it immediately for an amount determined by the judge. He also provided an "acceptable" lesser offer. I should get informed of the real estate agent, the lawyer conducting the sale and all marketing procedures. If any of the parties did not accept the lesser offer, would move to the "first refusal" option. Imagine my betting possibilities without money. Unfortunately, until today Michael continues to keep me in the dark about any details involving the sale of the property. The judge was now recognizing the preemptive right, also known as "first refusal". But, had denied it to the other legal shareholder with rights protected and bound by Guatemalan corporate laws.

Regarding the chattels from the Hong Kong apartment: Remember when I had to source money to pay the removal company in Hong Kong because Michael refused to do it at the last minute? When the shipment arrived in England, I had to pay extra for the content to get stored in the removal company's facility. After three months, and no home to take them to, the removal company couldn't keep my container any longer. So, I had to source alternative long-term storage with money from friends. The vast debt remains pending, and I am paying only the high-interest charges on my credit card and monthly storage fees to obey the orders of District Judge Mulkis to give Michael 50% of the chattels. I find the level of neglect from the court and my legal advisors unbearable.

CHAPTER 10: FRAUD, PERJURY AND MOCKERY

Then, in the February 2019 court hearing, Michael came up with a nonsensical new claim to torture me further; accusing me without evidence that I had his books and an artwork piece he referred to as his Chinese painting. The judge immediately added the items to the list I had to hand over to Michael, plus 50% of the chattels from the Hong Kong shipment. The family piano was also claimed in court by Michael as our daughter's possession. Michael arranged three removals when he took our daughter from the family home. The movers came and packed all her belongings, furniture and whatever she and Michael wanted to take. Conveniently, Michael left behind the family piano; now he wanted it back in one of his typical tantrums. So as per District Judge Mulki's orders, I have to ship it to any destination Michael decides. These items seem like nonsense to many, but it was no less than unbelievable when the same court that had left me homeless without evidence now imposes an even greater economic burden that is impossible for me to execute.

I wasn't sure if I should buy comic books to pass onto Michael instead as his books and draw a stickman on a big canvas; otherwise, I would need a magic wand. I offered evidence that Michael in September 2017 ordered two big international removals from Hong Kong to London with AGS, the same company I utilized for the overseas shipment. He distributed all his personal belongings. I have the list of content shipped in the two loads, one by air and for the large items, by sea, leaving no personal belongings behind. The judge ignored the cost of the Hong Kong removal and storage fees. My claims went into a vortex that no one wanted to approach.

District Judge Mulkis assigned himself to handle any other details dealing with the *Hieb* vs *Hieb* legal matter. Both parties should apply to the court of the said Judge on the first instance concerning the implementation of the orders. The judge varied his final order several times and added recitals. It was not until later that I learned recitals could not get appealed. Michael was to keep me informed of his efforts to find further employment. Also, notify me within seven days of becoming employed, and receive a copy of the employment agreement. But, of course, that did not happen.

After the December final court hearing, the judge refused my petition for permission to appeal and stay his orders. This left me without any of the family money or spousal maintenance. The orders of District Judge Mulkis meant nothing in Guatemala unless they first got legitimized and passed the scrutiny of the court observing Guatemalan law. Michael's tantrums and the imperialist way of thinking of the court of England didn't work there anymore. Yes, the suggestion had been passed for a case to get transferred or at least be followed up in Guatemala, but of course, Michael wanted nothing to do with it. His claims would have to pass the legal test of accuracy, and he knew that with falsifications, he had no chance. So, the company's legal representatives communicated that my interest as a shareholder was severely compromised. My actions in London endangered the stability and well-being of the company and the other shareholder.

CHAPTER 10: FRAUD, PERJURY AND MOCKERY

After the last day of court in December 2018, I exited the family court building feeling destroyed. Outside, Michael and I crossed paths. We were heading in opposite directions. He was laughing as he walked and talked on his mobile phone. He saw me and looked to the floor, avoiding my eyes. It must be horrid to be willfully so evil and live with the harrowing feeling that one day you will have to pay for your wrongs.

My health was in terrible shape. I suffered constant anxiety attacks, depression, and severe insomnia. My son David had moved back to New York. In London, alone and feeling broken, I decided to called him asking for his help. Not yet ready to disclose the outcome of the final court hearing, I promised to explain later. He asked me to fly to New York and spend Christmas with him and his fiancé.

A few days before I travelled, I found myself desperate, and feeling very lost. I had lost my daughter and didn't know how to tell the boys what Michael had done to derail the process of our divorce. Feeling I had nowhere to turn for help, I sat on the floor and cried like a baby. The sense of abandonment, loneliness and depression is a dangerous cocktail.

Suddenly, something warm began descending over my head, landing on my shoulders. Three times I heard, "EVERYTHING IS GOING TO BE FINE". An instant relief overwhelmed my mind and body. The kindness of that voice and the immediate effect is my conviction that a divine power was aware of my afflictions. To me it was a reassurance that I was not alone. The first thought that came to my mind was "the answer is love". Because when you love, you don't cheat or hate, kill, steal or be jealous. It was a wake-up call to realize that eventually, everything would be fine, and I had to make faith and love the foundations for the roots for me to overcome.

I remember packing my bag before Christmas and taking a train to the airport. I must have looked so sad and desperate that a gentleman stood up, walked towards me and asked if I was alright.

"Anything I can do to help?", he asked.

In desperation, I said, "Do you know a detective or anyone in the media? I need to expose a massive case of fraud."

"Sorry", the gentleman replied, "I'm afraid I don't. I am an architect but here is my business card—do get in touch if you need my help and I will do my best to assist".

He went back to his seat and a few stops later he got off the train. I feel immense gratitude for this gentleman's kind gesture.

Chapter 11

In the Land of Nothingness

I don't recall getting on the plane. My brain was in a trance until I heard the landing announcement.

For the first time, I was not even close to the strong woman David remembered. I held on to my son like a newborn to his mother. Queen and King, the two chihuahua doggies, were getting familiar with me when my daughter-in-law arrived. I slept like a rock the first night, feeling safe and loved. The following morning my son and I went for a walk; I recounted what had taken place in court. In disbelief, David listened attentively.

"Mom, remain calm", he said; "Evil people like Michael never win".

When I feel desperate and exhausted, I think of David's words.

In the evenings, once alone in my room, I would cry. Little King would leave his bed and scratch under my door to get in. He would come in and curl next to the bed, looking at me as if to say, "Don't worry, I am here". King would leave the room when he saw me sleeping. His tiny paws touching the wooden floor alerted me when he headed back to his bed on the first floor. It's incredible how a little creature could offer so much love to a stranger while human beings can be so vile.

During my stay in New York, I received a phone call from Michael. I had already blocked him from his other numbers but forgotten Skype. He asked me to leave things alone and how they were because bad things happened to people like me. I hung up and called the Metropolitan Police in London. I told them about Michael's aggressive behavior and that I had recently divorced him. I was given a reference number and advised to get in touch on my return to London.

As soon as I returned home, I called the police with the reference number. The police requested my permanent address; I didn't have any. So, I gave my son's address, his house was in the process of getting sold, and I had the keys. The Met Police transferred me to a local police station. A policeman proposed a visit a few hours later, and I accepted. A single police constable came to the house. He asked many questions and took a statement on a tablet. I expressed concern for my wellbeing and mentioned the kidnapping threats from Michael, the issues in court and the fraud. Constable Gascogne took a statement and provided a reference number; he also shared his email address. He said that a report needed to get generated and filed and for me to wait for the report number.

CHAPTER 11: IN THE LAND OF NOTHINGNESS

I waited two weeks, but no news from Gascogne, so I made my way to the police station. At the front desk, I gave them the reference number I had, and I asked for him. My reference number seemed to mean nothing. The policewoman tending the front desk couldn't find my complaint. I was told a message would get passed to him and for me to wait for a callback. A week later, I called again; the police station had no idea of such a reference. Disappointingly, the front desk told me that no personal messages would get passed to police officers. I waited one more week, but still no updates on my complaint. So, I paid another visit to Sutton Police Station. The person at reception informed me that Constable Gascogne had hurt an arm, and he was off duty that week. Once again, I was asked to wait until he got back to me. A couple of weeks later, I paid another visit to the police station. I received all kinds of excuses, including him not being in the area, not on duty, busy, etcetera. I returned to the police station a few more times and sent an email too. They said he would get back to me, but it never happened.

Michael knew our son's address in Sutton, making my temporary stay at David's place unsafe. Twice I was followed from the train station, but I returned to the taxi rank and boarded a taxi instead of walking. I became very aware of my surroundings and constantly checked over my shoulder. A friend receiving my post complained about men frequently showing at her place looking for me. They insisted on my address. Some said to have something for me. I did not dare go to familiar places or areas Michael and I lived in before moving to Hong Kong. During court appointments, I would apply for someone to escort me around the building and on my way out. I would take different routes to the underground and sometimes switch for a bus ride. I tried to disappear, hoping my legal matter soon resolved.

In January 2019, Jamie, my barrister, filed for permission to appeal, followed by appeal. Finally, the court date came to us, 26 July 2019, seven months of agonizing waiting. I requested my solicitors to help me find a way to get maintenance until the appeal. My legal team brushed me off and told me that there was nothing they could do except wait. I was desperate; I didn't have much money to make me last a month, never mind seven months. It was upholding how no one seemed concerned about my situation. My family in Guatemala were the only ones worrying and helping in whichever way they could. They were all disgusted by how the court and my legal team had managed my divorce matter. My older brother had recurring cancer and had more significant problems. Still, he was always there to speak with me while I cried over the phone.

At the beginning of the year, I received the money for my shares. I informed my solicitors and put the $69,000 USD to the disposition of the judge and the other party. The corporate lawyer had informed me and both sets of solicitors about Corporate law and the rights of shareholders and their intentions to exercise their right to first refusal. But the solicitors did not take her seriously. It was also clear that during a shareholders' meeting, when preforming shares transactions, the Board sets the value. Never before had Michael complained about the shares'

CHAPTER 11: IN THE LAND OF NOTHINGNESS

legal value until the final court hearing. Because if all things are not the way Michael wants, he will bend reality to make them his way. He was about to throw a tantrum and set war on me again. I'm not sure how his legal team could get court appointments in days, if not hours, but they managed it to push their agenda swiftly.

The other shareholder was entitled to protect her rights and stop the attempts of fraud threatening her interest. My solicitors from Vardags were in contact with the corporate lawyer overseeing the foreign company's interest in Guatemala. She often explained the local law and the unsettling directions of District Judge Mulkis to Terrence and Maria. They also had multiple opportunities to ask the lawyer questions. So, here we were with my legal team acting as if they were deer blinded by headlights.

Michael's legal team kept threatening to imprison me. As per their claims, I had violated court orders. Barrister Nicholas Wilkinson did not make a circle square; instead, he became an instrument to mislead the court and mess up what could have been a civilized legal matter.

Michael received his bonus compensation in January 2019 and conveniently ignored sharing his US tax filings with my legal team. He also neglected to share copies of missing bank accounts, balances, a formal letter of dismissal from HR, and disclosure in his compensation package. His legal team claimed Michael was not obliged to produce any more information. My legal team needed it for the Appeal.

In January, I felt as if I was in a battle zone. District Judge Mulkis stated that I had breached his worldwide freezing injunction of 19 December by allowing the other shareholder to perform her preemptive right for acquisition even though it was not my doing. Furthermore, my family had begun to distance themselves from me; a sentiment of guilt invaded me. My loved ones were getting hurt by my divorce. I was putting them in danger and closer to a monster I knew was capable of anything out of greed.

Without having an opportunity to agree or disagree, a general agreement was drafted in the form of an order by the judge. It read that "we" agree not to institute proceedings against each other under the Married Women's Property Act of 1882; Law Property Act of the Trust of Land, and the Appointment Trust Act of 1996.

All joint accounts were to be closed by Michael before 26 February 2019. By then, the list had shrunk from the original list of existing mutual banks and credit card accounts. Towards the last week of November 2019, I received a few insignificant deposits from Michael into my UK bank account. Despite insisting on formal evidence confirming the closure of the said accounts, I never received anything else, but an email from Michael.

District Judge Mulkis made several modifications to his final judgement by adding further orders and recitals when the other party wanted to push their agenda. Michael and his solicitors complained about me taking too long to sign the share transfer documents. On several occasions, my solicitors were reminded by Payne Hicks Beach that there was the penalty of imprisonment against me, which would get pursued if I remained uncooperative.

CHAPTER 11: IN THE LAND OF NOTHINGNESS

Anxiety attacks kept me awake for days on end. The other party through a tantrum, declaring I was in contempt of court. A court hearing got scheduled for 8 February 2019. In this hearing, the judge extended my time to sign the share transfer to 22 February. Please understand how you would feel if a judge asked you to commit fraud and threatened you with imprisonment if you did not obey? My solicitors informed the court that I was searching for the advice of a corporate and criminal lawyer in Guatemala. It was written in the document containing the orders of the judge that:

> "If the provision of any of this information is likely to incriminate the respondent [meaning me], they may be entitled to refuse to provide it, but it is recommended to take legal advice before refusing to provide the information."

During the court hearing of 8 February, a "General Financial Order" was issue. District Judge Mulkis wrote that I had accepted, was in complete satisfaction, and in an agreement with the terms of his new order. I don't know where my lawyers were; they didn't even object. I, for sure, was not in agreement with any of the terms. In this hearing, the judge made to benefit Michael further. The preposterous modification order included for Michael to choose the piano shipment's destination at my expense. According to District Judge Mulkis, this was called a clean break of capital and income. He ordered for me to pay Michael's legal fees for the court appearance.

The art of coaxing me was relentless, but I was determined not to jump from a bridge or in front of a passing train.

February was particularly tough for me. On the 22nd I got forced to sign over to Michael and his mother, Sharon Inglis, a property not legally mine, via a "share transfer" document in Spanish. Michael's legal team threatened me with confinement if I did not meet the deadline. In his order, District Judge Mulkis required me to legalize the share transfer with a notary. I felt scared. The warnings of the criminal and corporate lawyers in Guatemala rang in my head like deafening bells; I was committing fraud and now, legalizing it! I could not claim later, not knowing what I did. I roamed London like a lioness looking for prey. My hands shook every time I dialed the phone number of a notary's office. I had little money and expected to pay for the service; what a torture. When asked to provide details about the document needing notarization, the same question popped up; why are they in Spanish? And then, the "Nays" would pour, or the prices would hike astronomically. Finally! I found one good soul willing to see me on the same day and curious to inspect the papers. The gentleman was able to translate the content and, after several questions, felt comfortable to stamp it. I thanked the gentleman for being fair and genuinely concerned about my nervous twitching during our brief encounter. After notarizing the share transfer documents, District Judge Mulkis had ordered my solicitors to verify and certify them.

Michael hid from the court of England in his multiple failed attempts to register the company with the aid of the

CHAPTER 11: IN THE LAND OF NOTHINGNESS

"share transfer" documents and the orders of District Judge Mulkis, hence obstructing our legal process and distribution of wealth. Previously, he had untruthfully insisted the share transfers would immediately grant him a takeover of the company and property in Guatemala; consequently, District Judge Mulkis coaxed me to sign.

The corporate lawyer in Guatemala became aware of Michael and his local lawyer's illegal activities. So, they called me warning and hoping I would alert the court and for it to scrutinize the duo. I informed my solicitors and shared the evidence provided, but my solicitors from Vardags claimed it wouldn't make any difference because the judge had made up his mind. Further, evidence from Guatemala was insufficient to make any claims; why not at least present my argument. But challenging Vardags, I told Terrence that the court was receiving inaccurate information from Michael about the accounts taking place in Guatemala; why not at least present my argument? The reply felt like a bucket of ice water.

"District Judge Mulkis doesn't like you and is now favoring Michael, so delivering your argument would only further exacerbate your case with the judge".

How can it be possible that a legal firm shrugged their shoulders to corruption and discrimination? It is repulsive to me; the system needs to change because a broken legal system can only produce broken results.

When Michael and his local lawyers realized the impossibility of accomplishing what they claimed certain to the judge in England, Oscar Estuardo Paiz Lemus came up with another scam. Without evidence, Michael complained to the Judge that I was getting in the middle of him taking over the company. So, on 13 March 2019, he and his lawyer Paiz Lemus stated that the share transfer document was no longer enough. And that a shareholder's meeting in England was necessary.

It seems that my solicitors forgot I had no monetary resources; still, they insisted I should seek advice from a criminal lawyer in Guatemala. So once again, I went on a crusade to find a loan. A Guatemalan lawyer took pity on me and made me promise to repay if her advice would go over the small amount in deposit. The proficient lawyer spoke Korean and Spanish, she studied my matter, On 15 March, lawyer Ana Silvia urged me not to sign any document pushed by Michael and his lawyer. She prepared and sent my solicitors in London a detailed long list of the political and business constitution of the country. First, there was the absolute need to have a court hearing in Guatemala to make the proper determinations. The advice of the lawyer was translated to English and studied by my legal team in London. Terrence, the principal solicitor found some of the advice controversial because explicitly called what District Judge Mulkis was doing fraud and requested a shorter version of the content. He stated that he will use the information later in the process, but never did. Sadly, I wasn't even hoping for the judge to read it anyway. My legal team also had all the necessary information sent by the corporate lawyer back in December 2018 and then January 2019. But, Terrence decided not to prepare arguments with the useful legal information. When I heard the news of the intentions to execute a shareholder's

CHAPTER 11: IN THE LAND OF NOTHINGNESS

meeting in London, I asked, what about the other shareholder? I learned it would only be District Judge Mulkis, Michael's solicitors and me. The Guatemalan criminal lawyer had already strongly advised against not signing any document regarding the property. I felt Michael's new request pushed me further into legal problems with the Guatemalan criminal court. So, I decided not to partake and asserted that if the judge or Michael's legal team wanted to jail me, they should do so. It was frustrating and demoralizing to see my legal team's lack of action and not follow my instructions.

Irony

As per Guatemalan law, a shareholders meeting and its members, needed to be physically present in Guatemala. Oscar Estuardo Paiz Lemus knew this detail but concealed it from the judge. I communicated the fact and pleaded to my legal team from Vardags to argue the important detail, but I found only deaf ears. The audacity of holding a shareholders meeting in England, with documents in Spanish, took place on 2 May when District Judge Mulkis signed a resolution for Michael and his mother, Sharon Inglis, to be the 100% new shareowners of the company and property in Guatemala. Payne Hicks Beach witnessed the judges' signature and sent the document to get stamped with international certification from a convention of the AYA, which legalized international documents. None of the shareholders nor the corporate lawyers were present or informed that District Judge Mulkis would signed the resolution.

During the signing of the "shareholder meeting", Payne Hicks Beach solicitors told the judge that Michael had an airline ticket ready and needed to fly urgently to Guatemala. Suggesting a time constraint, so the document went into express-expediting mode. But instead, two days later, after signing the documents, Michael flew from London to Colombia, relaxed there, and then flew to Guatemala. The irony of it all.

When in Guatemala, photos and witness testimony corroborated that Michael's mistress Lina Hall waited outside a red car adjacent to the property. Michael, Oscar Estuardo Paiz Lemus, and Juan Carlos Velasquez unleashed privately hired armed police in front of the property in Guatemala. At the same time, three other men were by force, violating the main entrance door locks. Meanwhile, Michael and his local lawyer threatened the 11-year-old housekeeper's son, passing by the property to collect money from his mother and a set of keys. Screams and threats spewed by Michael and his cluster of thugs threatened to send Nilda, the housekeeper, to jail for trespassing on private property. When she tried to pass the keys to her son from one of the windows, Michael took the keys from her hand and kept them, leaving the child shaking from fear.

In distress, Nilda called the lawyers, my family and me via WhatsApp pleading for help. But what could I do from London? My sister was in the hospital with her son and my mom with relatives. The local lawyers decided to

CHAPTER 11: IN THE LAND OF NOTHINGNESS

send a representative to make a statement of account. Michael kept flagging documents in English signed by District Judge Mulkis.

"The court in England granted me this property; I am the owner." Michael shouted in the street,

"Get the people in the house out! They are trespassing!"

The commotion attracted local police, who were confused. Michael "convinced" them to help him. Meanwhile, neighbors were watching, calling family and friends to alert them about the turmoil. When Michael forced his entry into the property, Nilda ran to collect private documents and valuables and put them in a cardboard box to protect them, but Michael snatched them from her hands. As a result, a criminal was now in possession of confidential documents to the company; bank statements, corporate and personal bank cards, my mom's doctor's appointment cards, and my and the housekeeper's national IDs, which were always at the house in Guatemala.

Michael hijacked the property and threatened the housekeeper with incarceration. Lawyers defending the property and people in the house have videos of Michael and his two local lawyers chasing Nilda out of the house and in the street for about a block.

The lawyer who came to take the statement of account remained outside the property after the incident. She could hear Michael, Lina, the lawyers, and two bodyguards laughing inside the property. The housekeeper returned with her daughter to request her government ID and the set of keys. She only received her ID, but not before getting insulted and threatened. Nilda has an ongoing legal criminal case against Michael and his two lawyers in the Guatemalan tribunals in charge of defending women's rights.

After that incident, I lost my family's confidence. None of them wanted to speak with me. I've caused so many problems because of Michael's greed and our divorce. According to several family members, I had been unsuccessful in proving and defending my points in the Court of England and defending myself. They couldn't understand the level of corruption I was dealing with. It is not often when I try to analyze Michael's behavior. Still, when I do, I am amazed to recall the level of fraud and criminality he has chosen to embark on.

My relatives received their fair share of harassment, threats, and intimidation from Michael and his ruffians in Guatemala. My sister's son's front door was banged and kicked by two men driving a black or red car. Police attended several times but stopped visiting the property after many complaints. My nephew also complained about getting followed to and from the university by the same men. One day, he returned home from university; scared and not feeling well, he collapsed a few minutes later. An ambulance transferred him to a small local clinic that did not administer the necessary tests to catch any suspicious substance in his body. He later got transferred to a large hospital. His young life became suspended in a coma for over nine months; regretfully, he never recovered. I tried very hard not to lose my mind over the incident. It has been difficult for me to confront my sister's pain after losing her only son.

A black pickup truck, two men on bicycles, or one on a motorcycle followed and chased the Nilda more than once until she had to change her route home every day. Ultimately, she got tracked down and ran over by a motorbike, pushing her into a stone rubble pile and sending her to hospital with a broken leg and a concussion. Her son, whose school was next to the property, was harassed in the street before boarding the bus home. The ordeal was an unending nightmare for whoever had challenged Michael and his dubious lawyer in Guatemala.

In panic, I reported the incidents to my solicitors from Vardags in London. But my cries for help received little attention, and their comments unhelpful and dismissive;

"That's happening in another country Diana, there is nothing we can do".

Not sure if I can express in words what I felt when hearing their useless replies. I often try to remove negative thoughts from my mind. Their actions are theirs to face in their book of life.

Action Fraud

In 2019, a man phoned me out of the blue asking to verify my name.

"Who are you? Why do you have my number?" I asked.

He did not reply. He said he had something for me and that I needed to tell him where to find me. I hung up and called my solicitors in panic. Their instructions were to head home, inform the police and change my phone number. I could not afford to change my phone number but blocked all calls from unknown callers. I went to the Metropolitan Police; they sent me to Action Fraud, who proved to be a useless resource, if I could even call them a "resource". I was not taken seriously and pushed to file different complaints to "dissect" my multiple allegations. A few months later, a scandalous article got published about Action Fraud, with untrained people taking the calls of desperate citizens reporting fraud. The person taking the call would laugh at the victim calling and mock them in a video which went viral during the report.[19]

I began hiding and looking over my shoulder. Finally, a friend agreed to receive my mail. Her family were also victims of Michael's harassment. Strange men will show up at her place, demanding to speak with me. When confronted, they insisted on having something for me that needed to be delivered directly. Where is she? We need her address. My friends directed them to my solicitors, but the men insisted that they would come back unless they told them where I was.

Displaced

Before the appeal, I went from sofa to sofa until I ran out of friends who could help. I had so much on my mind,

CHAPTER 11: IN THE LAND OF NOTHINGNESS

and my morale was low. Then, asking for advice, a friend mentioned a place that provided help for abused women. I found the details and began calling every day until one day I got an appointment. After hearing my story, I went on a waiting list for shelter accommodations. After a few weeks, I finally got allocated a small room. I immediately made the place my home. I cleaned the walls, floors and windows, washed old curtains and thanked God for a roof over my head. At the place were living women from all different backgrounds: women from Pakistan, Eritrea, Portugal and Brazil; Christians and Muslims; a Venezuelan trans-sexual, and a Cuban girl who had been there for two years who was now an Agnostic Guatemalan. There were also a few children.

We shared the kitchen and common areas. There were strict rules on what to do and when to do it. Cameras blanketed the inside of the building. The manager was a bitter and moody woman from Brazil who made sure we remembered who the boss was. Later, I found that the shelter charged a hefty sum per person and the differences between what we were to receive and what we got.

Most of us did not have money to use the dryer, and on rainy days, it was impossible to dry on the patio. Despite explanations, we were ordered not to air dry in the laundry room. The trans-sexual person from Venezuela, named Blondie, would keep voodoo dolls in the freezer, and when others complained, the manager would get nasty. I believe that the refuge wanted to tap into monetary resources from other organizations. Keeping a trans-sexual man in the refuge for abused women allowed them to file for such grants. He had come from Spain claiming abuse. I asked him why he applied for help in London and not Spain? He blandly responded that England did not check for facts. When observing my situation, I often thought, how could Michael feel carefree about his crimes? I guess he also knew Blondie's trick.

I got along well with all the tenants. I speak some Portuguese, so I managed to very quickly mingle with the Brazilian girls who didn't speak much English. Until today, I am still in touch with two of them. I often helped the lady from Eritrea and her two children. We used to chat during what I called the midnight coffee hour for those who could not sleep from worry. I would make tea or coffee and tell them funny stories so that we could laugh a little. I would go between Spanish, Portuguese and English with the same silly joke. The Muslim girl had a hard time in a place that cooked pork and with the transsexual man for obvious reasons. Hence, the poor girl had no freedom except in her tiny room, where I often played with the baby.

The Cuban woman got trafficked as a sex slave to Europe. Having managed to escape, she flew to England, ending up in this shelter. Still, after two years and no perspective to solving her legal status, she ran away. Her mother in Cuba needed money to keep supporting her son. My heart broke when I learned about her story. I felt angry and powerless for not being able to help her.

Several of us got robbed in the refuge. Only three people had keys to our rooms; the manager, the cleaning woman and the tenant. Several of us got robbed in the refuge. Only three people had keys to our rooms; the manager, the person who cleaned the office area and the tenant. I lost a precious gift saved for my daughter's birthday, my handbag and a pair of shoes. In addition, one Brazilian lady lost her wedding ring and another a piece of jewelry belonging to her daughter living with her in the refuge.

I was outspoken and requested a police report and review camera recordings. I never got see the film, and the manager insisted on typing and sending the police report for me. I never heard from the police.

While in the shelter, I was still fighting my case in the family court. My luggage served me as a desk. The crying of the children would keep me from concentrating. A woman next door had attempted suicide and constantly spoke to herself, moaning and crying most of the time. I used to invite her for short walks so she would leave her room. It was all I could do at the time. She told me her husband had abandoned her and, in her world as a Muslim woman, she was nothing without him. It was so sad to hear that the creators of life and once the pinnacle of society were now second-class citizens, or worse, nothing, when there wasn't a man in their life.

My solicitors weren't getting any money from me, and the time for appeal was ticking. As if they had never heard before that the property was not mine, they decided to speak with lawyers in Guatemala about me signing a loan over the foreign property benefiting Vardags. I sought advice from my lawyer in Guatemala; Ana Silvia asked who the legal firm was. Her immediate reply brought shivers down my spine. Ana Silvia urged me not to get involved with such a legal firm and not sign anything unless there was a court order in Guatemala. News links Ana Silvia sent proved her concerns. The legal firm chosen by Vardags was an imminent danger. News cited the firm criminally investigated for working in obtaining illegal visas for questionable Russian citizens. Now more undesirable people knew about my matter and the contested wealth. The company and the property put my family and me in-danger of extortion.

July was approaching, and with it, the appeal. Three days before the court appointment on 26 July 2019, my solicitors abandoned me. With our court bundle already filed, Vardags sent a letter to the court giving notice that I would be self-representing. On the first day of the appeal, I presented myself with an in-person request to postpone the litigation so I could find legal aid. The appeal judge was His Honor Judge Everall QC.

I was ignorant of the topic and thought I could get public defense for a civil matter. As it turns out, I was wrong. It is easy to get legal aid in criminal court, but I had to pay for civil matters such as divorce. I could not wrap my head around the concept, but there is so much I don't understand about English law.

Judge Everall pointed out I was not successful in securing the services of my legal team, never mind successful in finding legal aid. The other party's legal team claimed I had orchestrated the whole thing—they were a group of delusional bullies. Judge Everall denied my petition to adjourn the appeal. I got told that I looked intelligent and competent enough to face it independently. My ex-

CHAPTER 11: IN THE LAND OF NOTHINGNESS

solicitors had already sent the court bundle, so I was to use it, aiding me in following proceedings. It was either accepting the comments of HH Judge Everall or declaring myself mentally incompetent.

Not even in my nightmares did I see myself in such a bad situation. With no legal representation and ignorant of the law, facing Michael and his legal team was pure cruelty. Looking into the empty space behind the judge's bench, I said to myself, "Keep your mind, remain respectful and do your best as this fight is not just for you."[20]

I have learned that life is challenging, and that good and not so good experiences help. They provide lessons to enrich our life experiences. The more we get used to our reality, the faster we can achieve inner peace and wisdom. But if we resist, whatever we fear, will persist.

On the first day of court, the other party submitted a non-agreed court bundle, a highly unorthodox move to say the least. I didn't have enough time to inspect it—most documents were in Spanish. Michael's barrister, Nicholas Wilkinson, spoke first. Without evidence he argued that despite my alleged interference with his client, Michael still acquired the company and property in Guatemala. One of his exhibits showed a blown-up copy of my passport. He reiterated that, as previously stated by District Judge Mulkis, I was a liar because I had told the court that I didn't have a passport. Pictures of inside the house, dirty dishes in the kitchen, beds undone in several bedrooms, towels in several bathrooms and cloths in the closets. I think Michael forgot his argument in the court of District Judge Mulkis back in December that no one lived on the property. The exhibits were solely to ask the court for me to pay for the cleaning service because my family or people renting the property had left the house dirty. Michael was contradicting himself. But to this, the court did not seem to care or have not read the arguments of my claims. It was a miracle my family wasn't on the property when Michael highjacked it. Flory was in hospital tending her sons delicate health state my mom with relatives. My mother would have had a heart attack with all the commotion.

In the same court bundle were documents signed by an overnight judge on duty or Justice of the Peace. Michael claimed that such a judge had granted him permission to occupy the property and legally awarded him the company. I took notes as fast as I could in a small green book. My stomach revolted with desperation to scream and say something to the judge. But kept quiet and waited for my turn.

I explained to Judge Everall that the passport was the same expired passport known during the final court hearing of December. Also, a Justice of the Peace in Guatemala, England or any other part of the world wouldn't have such capacity, primarily because of civil and corporate law differences. Oscar Estuardo Paiz Lemus said that the company had been successfully registered on Michael's name, issued new shares, and took over the property. Michael and his lawyers did not provide significant details on how they achieved the above madness.

There is an advanced ongoing criminal investigation in Guatemala vs Michael and his lawyer Oscar Estuardo

CHAPTER 11: IN THE LAND OF NOTHINGNESS

Paiz Lemus. Unfortunately, due to the pandemic, criminal court cases are taking longer to resolve. In documents presented to the corporate registrar's office, the pair claimed to have a shareholder meeting in Guatemala. The criminal investigators are puzzled as to how Michael and Paiz Lemus made the changes of ownership issuing new company shares. Allegations of fraud against the above men, include the investigation over the original shareholder's rights, documents provided by the pair, and the lack of record indicating the Corporate Registrar's office receiving the original share certificates to proceed with the transfer and issued new ones in favor of Michael and his mother. This matter also under the scrutiny of the law. It is necessary to cite that Oscar Estuardo Paiz Lemus happens to be the second speaker on the board of directors for the Business Institute of Legal Mercantile Law. Corrupt collaborators within the Corporate Registrar Bureau? Most probably yes.

Michael also managed to buy the corporate accountant who facilitated him with privilege company documents. Criminal investigations are also taking place against the Justice of the Peace, whom Michael claimed entitled him with the full rights of the company to takeover of the property, and against Carol Janet Aroche Pineda, the prosecutor, who is said to have interfered with the investigation conducted by the corporate and criminal lawyers in Antigua, Guatemala.

A travel ban got issued against Michael. He is known to travel with two passports to confuse his entries and exits by using US passports to enter and leaving with a British one. It is believed he replaced them both, as he knew that we had the details of his previous ones. So, at the moment, the immigration authority has been unable to track his entries. The criminal court called for Michael and his local lawyer to appear numerous times. But the duo played the postponing game, and the pandemic helped with the delays, but not for long.

How did a bundle in Spanish get presented as evidence to a judge in England who doesn't speak Spanish, and when the official language of the country is English? And when the vast majority of the documents were untranslated, except those which benefited Michael? Why were the documents translated and notarized by the same Paiz Lemus? Four years later, I am still waiting for the answers.

Going back to the appeal day, I remember requesting Judge Everall to observe the dubious documents presented by the other party. The judge agreed about the Justice of the Peace not having the power to do what Michael and his legal team claimed.

So, let's stop and analyze the twist of the legal permitting illegalities. Why wouldn't the Judge question the false account? Why not get Michael's legal team to explain? I have observed how the other party's defense hides under remarks such as, "My client provided evidence; I have the right to believe him."

But where is the truth in such a statement? I firmly believe legal firms should be held accountable for scrutinizing evidence provided by their clients, thus, helping the family court to deal with only verified information and

CHAPTER 11: IN THE LAND OF NOTHINGNESS

saving precious court time and resources. Only fair trials can yield equitable outcomes.

Among my arguments were that Michael had lied about the date he got dismissed from work. In addition, I never received a formal confirmation with details from his previous employer and tax filing disclosures. I brought up the issue about the expired power of attorney. I felt that by presenting my findings, I could finally disprove Michael's false claims. I also provided evidence about the correct antiquity of the property from the official Property Registrar's Bureau, demonstrating that it was only 70 years old in 2018. Unfortunately, Judge Everall felt that my arguments had already been dealt with in the court of District Judge Mulkis. I could not believe that only I was interested in questioning Michael's about his shady activities.

We got to the end of three painful days of the appeal. I lost and got ordered to pay hundreds of thousands of British Pounds for Michael's legal fees. Appeals are highly technical in the law; everybody in the courtroom except me knew it. So, I had no chance to succeed. But, as to the judge, ignorance of the law is not an excuse. So, what if we say it how it is, and call it "Justice is for those who can afford it". For a person living in a refuge for abused women, the prospects of paying hundreds of thousands of pounds to a wealthy financier for his legal fees was appalling. Nevertheless, the judge called it fair.

If you think I was afraid of Michael before now, I was petrified and very concerned for my well-being after calling his fraud in court. Although Judge Everall did not seem to focus on the importance of what I was disclosing, the significance of my statements was massive. On the other hand, I know Michael was paying attention. As soon as I left the courtroom, I sought to apply for a non-molestation order.

It was confusing to find the way around the court and different buildings, pay fees (if required), and fulfil other prerequisites without knowing where to go. To add tension to the matter, no one ever told me I had to file my court bundle with evidence in specific places and dates before court appointments. Judges count on this information to hold the hearing and follow both parties' arguments. It was a long three years during my legal process of extensive learning while running around with over 20 kilos of documents in my rucksack, ultimately injuring my lower back.

I received the first appointment to apply for a non-molestation order 28 August. Three female magistrates and a court clerk led the hearing. Despite the court citation, Michael was not present. The court clerk advised the magistrates not to make any decisions because Michael was not there. Due to the nature of the application, it got suggested that a judge conducts the hearing. I received the appointment for late 5 September. Once again, Michael was not present. Judge James Bellamy QC became upset with me because I was not to rely upon the court notifications, something I did not know. I got dismissed and ordered to contract a private company to notify Michael. My explanation for the lack of monetary resources did not

CHAPTER 11: IN THE LAND OF NOTHINGNESS

get through to the judge. He replied that it was my responsibility.

My perspective is that some judges live in another world. They don't understand or want the trouble of understanding the problems faced by litigants in my situation. I had to provide court bundles without knowing how to prepare them or having the necessary software to do it. I needed to print a complete set of copies for the court, the other party and myself. Depending on the amount of evidence and documents, the cost was close to £100 plus binders. It was a nightmare carrying all the material back and forth. Finally, after several attempts from the professional document server, he managed to speak with a man who identified himself as the new tenant. Michael had moved months ago and neglected to notify the court. I had the feeling that it was a matter of time before Michael moved out of London. Once he began working again, it would serve him well if the British court could not see his income.

Information from relatives led me to Michael's location in Hong Kong. The law there required the server to get contracted by a legal firm. Luckily, the first legal firm I consulted in Hong Kong about my divorce accepted the job. Michael's solicitors in London confirmed he was served. Apparently, their client was furious by getting disturbed at 11:00 p.m. when returning from dinner.

The next court appointment was at the end of September. Michael was not present and his solicitors asked the court to excuse him. They could not say he was busy working, so the excuse was him leaving abroad. Once again, I was self-representing. Michael's legal team was Ben-Parry Smith and Barrister Ben Wooldridge. The other side follows the usual mission; to rely on trashing me. I was portrayed as jealous in the hearing because Mr. Hieb had moved on and started another life with his new partner. I could observe the judge getting trapped in the web of lies from Michael's legal team. No one seems to remember it was me who filed for divorce. How jealous could I be if the man I despised was finally gone?

I asked the judge to consider the narrative of the incriminating audio; the Skype call from Michael's phone number, a police report from Hong Kong, the conduct and fraud statements filed in during divorce proceedings; pictures of physical abuse and my worries after the appeal.

As the judge became more concerned with my statement, he began to quiz Michael's legal team. The two looked at each other and exchanged whispers. Ben Wooldridge pointed out that the incidents may have happened in 2017 when the couple was going through the most challenging part of their separation. He also emphasized the happenings being out of time to be considered valid in court proceedings.

"Besides", Mr. Wooldridge said, "Our client, is now living in Hong Kong—what harm can he present to Mrs. Hieb?"

The judge asked me why didn't I report my concerns to the police in England. I confirmed doing so but did not get any help. I also mentioned the issue with Sutton police, the Metropolitan Police and Action Fraud. He was not impressed with what sounded like excuses. The judge

CHAPTER 11: IN THE LAND OF NOTHINGNESS

confirmed that I didn't have a report even though I had made complaints to the police. The time to present them as evidence had expired without a follow-up.

I felt a knot in my stomach when I noticed the face of joy in Michael's legal team. Ben Woolridge insisted for my application to get dismissed without merit. The judge agreed, and without waiting for my turn I jumped into the conversation in desperation and said, "Your honor, a criminal mind continues to be so even from afar. Even if Mr. Hieb lives in another country, he could hire someone to do the dirty business for him. What would you do, how would you feel if something happens to me?"

My case got dismissed without merit. My legs trembled, wishing for the earth to swallow me. I thought about the ineptitude of Constable Gascogne and how ignoring my pleas has cost me a reinforcement to keep me safe. Sadly, after reading atrocities about the Metropolitan Police in England, I realized that my case is not isolated.[21]

The following day, the judges' clerk sent a note; the verdict changed to "Extempore". It meant the door was ajar for me if I needed to escalate my petition for protection.

Chapter 12

Discrimination

Appealing the appeal; I don't mean to bore you with many legal procedures, but please bear with me, as they all have a purpose for documenting my story and will soon unveil their reasons. Brexit was about to take place. My plead to challenge the results of the appeal of July 2019 filed in October 2019. I received communication from the court in November and had no results until January 2020.

Worth Reading

Although there is no direct connection between the UK's membership of the ECHR and membership of the EU, Brexit could affect the protection of human rights in the UK. This is due to the decision to stop the EU Charter of

Fundamental Rights from taking effect after the UK leaves the EU.

The ECHR is an international treaty the UK signed in 1950. States that signed up committed to upholding certain fundamental rights, such as the right to life, the right to a fair trial and the right to freedom of expression. The HRA enables people to bring cases in UK courts in order to uphold their ECHR rights.

Suppose future security cooperation is to come anywhere near current levels of collaboration. In that case, the UK will likely need to commit to ongoing adherence to these standards. Accordingly, the Political Declaration proposes a "Broad, comprehensive and balanced security partnership" underpinned by continued adherence to the ECHR. The UK has not yet resumed talks about the subject to confirm its compliance with the ECHR.[22]

Attempting to expose what had happened during the appeal and the misestimation of Michaels' fraudulent conduct, I ask several sections of the family court of appeals for guidance on how to appeal the appeal. Some people took pity and provided minimal help, as they were not supposed to. The Family Court will not instruct you how to face proceedings, defend yourself, or which steps to follow if you have no clue which document to complete when self-representing. Legal firms, solicitors and barristers, especially in the Central Family Court, are part of a massive multi-million enterprise in London. If you don't know how to proceed then you will be walking on pins and needles to get to where you need to.

CHAPTER 12: DISCRIMINATION

Finally, I received directions toward the correct court and building: the High Court of Justice Family Division - Appeals. Clerks there greeted me with a mix of kindness and pity. After inspecting all documents were in order, the application fee paid, and required readings for the judge included, a court clerk allowed my documents to reach evaluation. Feeling accomplished, I went home and anxiously waited for feedback. Somehow, I lost my fear of stepping into court, with their dark hallways and gothic buildings. I was becoming a sort of court warrior.

Honorable Mr. Justice Williams reviewed my case and sent notes stating that HH Judge Everall had made recitals explaining his court did not have any jurisdiction to determine any appeal in respect of a Recital to an order. I could only appeal the cost of the appeal ordered by HHJ Everall QC. One thing was for sure, pursuing the second appeal, and losing it, would leave me paying further legal costs to the other party, in the range of £1,800 per hour. It was crushing, but I had to accept Honorable Mr. Justice William's information. As soon as I gained my composure, I began typing a thank you note to Mr. Justice Williams and clerk for the information. At the same time, I asked to withdraw my application

I did not have the luxury to wait for Michael to do the right thing and returned what it was rightfully mine. It was crucial to prove that both companies where Michael invested hundreds of thousands of our money had not suffered the devastating losses he claimed. I also kept up the search for his current employment. The company's registrar and other online information showed no signs of catastrophic failures. Instead, I found Fintec articles praising both companies in England and Hong Kong for their fast growth in the past few years.

I was getting closer, and I think Michael could feel it. After several applications to the Central Family Court, Michael's suddenly declared he "quite recently" became employed. I was not allowed to know who the employer was. Michael's solicitors claimed that my behavior was dangerous and unacceptable. They could not release the employer's name just in case I would attempt to damage their client's "reputation".

According to Michael's legal team, their client didn't have to pay spousal maintenance. Despite taking possession of the company and property in Guatemala, he was still unsuccessful in selling it. But he said he would pay spousal maintenance out of the kindness of his heart. It was almost comical to hear such a statement. Still, by then, I was used to hearing absurdity in the family court.

It was impossible not to feel fed up with Michael's legal team's conduct. They had intentionally derailed a legal process and seemed comfortable with that. Finally, I had to resort to complaining to the head of the divorce department of Payne Hicks Beach, Mr. Phillip McGuirk. Unfortunately, he dismissed me by stating that he was satisfied that there was no misconduct on the part of any lawyer who is employed by PHB and that he did not consider it appropriate for me to correspond with him any further regarding this matter.

I found a way to move my complaint to the Solicitors Regulation Authority (SRA). And it was then that I discovered the colossal evil. There is much to say in a stream of criticism toward the "independent regulators", including those overseeing the conduct of judges, solicitors, barristers, the metropolitan police and the police regulators, but we will take a look at the SRA for now.

Legal firms are not being held accountable for their part in money laundering. According to MGI Midgley Snelling LLP,[23] chartered accountants "…call to protect compliance officers who report solicitors to SRA".[24]

Under enough pressure, the act of backdating a document, misleading a client, or hiding a mistake can seem like the only way out for an otherwise ethical lawyer. Through its recent thematic review, involving responses from over 200 solicitors, the Solicitors Regulation Authority has recognized a serious problem in law firms. I can only view this reference with the perspective that dishonest legal firms create dishonest employees.[25]

In October 2019, I launched my complaint to the SRA against Ben Parry-Smith and Joshua Moger from Payne Hicks Beach. It was a long process in which, between getting ignored and remaining persistent reached a pinnacle moment. Something considered worth looking into was found by one of the SRA's investigators. Since my complaint, several scandals have appeared in the news concerning the SRA. For example, in July 2020, was the case of a £33 million cover-up.[26]

I also had to trigger an investigation from the Legal Ombudsman to review Camilla Fusco, the solicitor from Anthony Gold. Among the list of complaints were ineptitude and ignoring her client's instructions. Six months later, the Legal Ombudsman replied that I had not followed their procedure and started again by complaining directly to the solicitor's firm first. I did so on 14 February 2020. Kim Beatson, partner, mediator & collaborative lawyer and Camilla's boss, replied to my query.

What happened with Anthony Gold is alarming. There is an absence of accountability and integrity within the organization regulating legal firms in the "divorce industry". Anthony Gold doctored documents in my case file to absolve themselves from the investigation and presented it in what they called the "evidence bundle."

Even sadder was the action the Legal Ombudsman took against me. I was lied to and betrayed; they insinuating that I was the one tampering with documents, and my investigation was dismissed without an equitable solution. My complaints were discarded. It is crushing when you get repeatedly victimized, especially when the oppressor knows you are vulnerable and have little opportunity to fight back. I highly recommend investigating the professional working standards of Ms. Sophie Hadley-Hall and Mr. Sidhu from the Legal Ombudsman for covering up the fraud. The correct word that comes to mind to describe Anthony Gold's behavior is "disgusting". I wish we never crossed paths.

On 5 November 2019, my complaint with the Legal Ombudsman against Stewarts Law was filed on the grounds of ignoring fraud, not following their clients' instructions, and letting a client's bill accumulate without pursuing a court order granting them the right to get paid by the other party. Also, for making me sign a document without explaining the content and denying legal representation. Once again, the Legal Ombudsman sent me to start my complaint as per their "way". I advocated for my complaints to keep their position in the queue. Not doing so would have amounted to at least a year before getting reviewed. Finally, on 7 May 2020, the process of looking into my matter began.

In October 2019, I filed my complaint with the Legal Ombudsman against Vardags on grounds of not following their client's instructions, neglecting to present evidence, allowing legal bills to accumulate to an astronomical amount and not pursuing payment as per court order, and abandoning me three days before the appeal. Vardags had sent a note to the court, with it a document with my signature, releasing them from legally representing me. I don't ever remember signing such a document and especially not three days before the appeal. Despite sending evidence to the Legal Ombudsman, where I explicitly complained to Vardags in writing, the Legal Ombudsman did not accept the format. Leaving no choice but to start again. So, I began my complaint process against Vardags in April 2020. I had already lost six valuable months, time much needed to keep working on steering my matter in the right direction. Vardags reacted nastily to our disagreement. Linda Cronin replied to my case, stating their complaint policy allowed them at least eight weeks to respond, following whatever time they took after the eight weeks to review and reply.

I also filed a complaint to the BAR standards against Barrister Nicholas Wilkinson in October 2019. The person reviewing my claims was Maithili Sreen. I received the reply stating they directed their resources to areas of significant risk to the public interest giving priority to such. They said that the BAR did not consider that Mr. Wilkinson had breached their Handbook stating that:

> "It may help if I explain that a barrister will advise his or her client in a way that protects and promotes their client's interests, but they ultimately act on their client's instructions. Unless they knew what they are saying or presenting to the court is false, they must act on their own client's instructions. In this case, there is no evidence that Mr. Wilkinson knew that anything he said was false. Accordingly, there is nothing to suggest Mr. Wilkinson's conduct gives rise to a potential breach of the Handbook. Another concern you raise is that Mr. Wilkinson presented an expired document or a document without a proper translation. However, I should explain that presenting an expired document or not providing a proper translation in and of itself doesn't amount to a potential breach of the BSB Handbook unless there is evidence of dishonesty or that the barrister sought to mislead the court."[27]

Call me crazy but those were precisely the main points of my complaint. Complaint: obstruction of justice and misleading the court. Different words, same meaning. Is that what is taught in law school? How to go around until you make your argument valid, even if it is not?

CHAPTER 12: DISCRIMINATION

On 24 March 2020, my subsequent complaint was again against Nicholas Wilkinson, including Mr. Joshua Viney, Junior Barrister from One Hare Court. To escalate my disapproval of the BAR dismissing my previous complaints, I raised objections to the BAR Conduct Review Unit. I highlighted the specifics of ethics, honesty and behavior, including victimizing and harassment breaches from the Handbook. I was alarmed when told that lying in court was not something that could get addressed as a complaint.

How much of a low life could you be to take advantage and victimize a vulnerable person? It is a brutal tactic adapted by bullies to attack the weak and lonely. So, line up and throw your punches because I may be alone, desperate and scared, but I am not going anywhere. Suited for the occasion, I share the following quote by Helen Keller:

> "Keep your face to the sunshine and you cannot see the shadows. It's what the sunflowers do."

This quotation encourages us to seek out the good, the positive, and the happy aspects of each day. Focusing on the positive and choosing to look for the best in life, no matter what life throws at us, helps to banish the shadows, which are the negative, unhappy thoughts. Despite being both deaf and blind, Helen spent her life thinking of other people and campaigning for other disabled children and adults. I invite you not to be afraid to question, and build the courage to fight for a better, fairer place.

Hold my hand; let's create an invisible chain; walk together and let's be relentless until we acquire it.

Eyes Windows of the Soul

And here was my ex-husband, who claimed poverty and unemployment for two years, but never dared to leave his ultra-expensive legal team. Imagine having the solicitors at Payne Hicks Beach at his service, representing Prince Charles in his divorce from the late Diana, Princes of Wales and Dubai Princess Haya. Princess Haya was also represented by Barrister Nicholas Wilkinson from One Hare Court. The eyes are the windows of the soul. I often wonder if Princess Haya saw in Mr. Wilkinson the same soul I saw? Your Honor, would you tell me one day?

I found myself in a rabbit hole, seeking help and trying to understand and get the correct interpretation of the law regarding the different orders, recitals, unless orders and judgements on my matter. I also went to organizations that promote helping victims of all types of abuse. Although some said to facilitate defending human rights, the telephone numbers listed would go unanswered and in a loop, sending the calls back to government helplines. If the phone ever answered, I had to invest hours on the phone just to find excuses and rejection.

I contacted the Legal Aid Society. After insisting and providing in-depth explanations and pleading for help, I qualified for a legal aid certificate. Then, with a code

CHAPTER 12: DISCRIMINATION

given, I searched and contacted legal firms from a long list that said to provide legal aid.

I called most if not all the firms listed. None wanted the certificate. Some of the firms requested private documents just to reject my case later. I heard excuses about not being enough solicitors taking divorce matters, the case being outside their expertise or too complicated. Some firms claimed they had already taken enough legal aid litigations. Other legal firms didn't seem to bother reviewing my documents when I placed follow-up calls. A brief description over the phone was enough for rejection, but not before offering help if I was willing to pay.

In one of the rare in-person appointments, the solicitor asked me to stop speaking. He told me that I sounded like someone trying to overthrow the government. I replied, "Sir, history has proven that seeking justice has been more difficult than changing a government regime."[28]

My attempts with the Direct Access barrister were fruitless and frustrating as well. Barrister G. Stanley charged me £2,160 GBP to review my documents to write a chronology of what had taken place in my legal matter. She then wrote a paragraph stating I would not succeed in any further appeal. Another barrister named Oji charged £200 per hour to tell me my case was too difficult.

Suppose, one of the litigants qualifies for a Civil Legal Aid certificate. In that case, the task for this poor soul is just the beginning. The client is obliged to research, contact and beg a legal firm to accept the certificate. It was demoralizing. At one point, I began to inquire how many cases each of the firms handled and how many clients have they helped in the last month or any given time during the current year. Communication stopped drastically after my inquiries. I never received any emails with statistics regarding my queries. If any of my readers ever contribute to organizations aiming to help victims of any type of charity, please ask for reports to identify where your money is going. Also, ask for the percentage of funds dedicated to the victims and specific numbers of individuals aided. The government should require quarterly, easy to understand statements of accounts and public records showing the number of cases handled by each organization. I think accountability is a must to ensure the money benefits the people who need it most.

Cutting My Wins or Rising Phoenix?

Michael continued with his dirty business in Guatemala. With newly issued shares and his name in the property registrar as owner, he and his friends from Century21 were not selling the house; instead, renting it as a luxury property and benefiting from the proceeds.

Michael had a circus going on, he and his local lawyer Oscar Estuardo Paiz Lemus continued getting criminally investigated. On the other hand, I was making desperate attempts to prove to the Court in England what was going on in Guatemala. All the information I received was enough to raise further questions about Michael's conduct and how he handled the property and the company.

CHAPTER 12: DISCRIMINATION

My subsequent court filing triggered a judgement summon to claim Michael owed me money. 16 March 2020 was set for the court appointment, a few days before my birthday. I compiled a good set of evidence bundles. There was already news about Covid-19 and a possible pandemic. Reflecting on the wave of disaster that took the world by storm, I have nothing but appreciation and sincere gratitude for all frontline and essential workers. They helped us get through the past two years of emergency, uncertainty and sadness.

Michael worked in Hong Kong and was living a lavish life, which I proved in my court bundle. His consulting company, Balham Core Ltd, which Michael claimed in the final court hearing of December 2018 to be essential to his livelihood, was left dormant. In attempts to conceal his work status, obtaining information was challenging but not impossible. Michael kept his profile hidden for a while until after the court appointment of 16 March, when he went on to show his shiny new positions.

During this court appointment, I provided documentation that on 29 April 2019, Gojoko Marketing Ltd. changed its name to Gojoko Credit Systems Ltd. But the plot thickened when I saw that Gojoko Systems Ltd moved to the same building as AMPLIFI. The majoritarian shareholder of Gojoko also happens to be a Director of AMPLIFI or ex-AMP Credit Technologies. AMP Credit Technology in Hong Kong had also changed its name in 2019 and was now AMPLIFI Holdings Ltd. Would I still be able to collect the money from both of the above companies, who owe me as per the court in

England? My above arguments did not impress the judge, and the court meeting swiftly moved to another topic. So here I am. But since I am not going anywhere soon, I will keep waiting for the day when crossroads collide and the time for disclosure comes. I need to see you all eye to eye.

The Wrong Judge

Looking back at my actions, I realized that it was less than helpful to request HH Judge Everall to lead the court hearing in March 2020. He conducted my appeal in July 2019 so I thought having a judge familiar with my legal matter would help expedite things. Judge Everall had previously witnessed fraudulent documents supplied by Michael, and I thought he would be pleased to see things advancing towards a fairer position.

Unfortunately, that was not the case. The court, barristers and solicitors are like a brotherhood; self-representing parties or clients are outsiders. From the very beginning of the session, I noticed how Judge Everall seemed frustrated with me.

He asked me if I was again self-representing while rolling over his eyes. I presented a bundle of over 300 pages of evidence and information to back up my claims. He said I had taken too long providing the court bundle and that it was too much information for him to read. The other party complained that I had taken until late the night before to share the information. They also complained that I had put a password in the documents. I

CHAPTER 12: DISCRIMINATION

replied it was read-only as I shared the court bundle by email the same way Michael's solicitors had done. But after their request, I had also shared the password for them to print. I knew all the content would end up in Michael's hands, and I had to limit the amount of tampering he could do before it got to the court.

I argued that the other party knew most of the information in the court bundle. I had also mentioned sending a notice of the problems I was experiencing with my old computer. It kept overheating, and two of the characters stopped working. It took me ages to compile the information and prepare a decent court bundle. Then I had to source the money to print the court material, close to £200 GBP. I explained to Judge Everall that the new information was not that much and that the rest were already know material used as exhibits to help support my points. I requested the judge to allow me to walk him through the bundle, and that I would use only the most crucial information from the material, but the judge declined my request.

For self-serving purposes, Michael's legal team forgot to tell the judge about our communication with my explanations. I looked like a fool in front of Judge Everall and was very little I could do in the few moments I was granted to speak. I was confident of the entitlements of at least a small percentage from the retirement funds. But barrister Joshua Viney and the solicitors from Payne Hicks Beach kept steering the judge into inflammatory statements against me. I could not understand, I had received advice from two legal firms. Both solicitors had inspected all court orders and documents, agreeing with my claims. Why was only when in court that things would turn upside down? The other party had a long list prepared to show I was only wasting the court's time. There was an exhibit of my statement from July 2018 to file a maintenance pending suit in their court bundle, a report prepared by Stewarts Law. The maintenance pending suit was never filed by Stewarts. And Michael's legal team knew it, but their intention was to misrepresent my character. My actions were wrongly depicted as antagonistic and called ridiculous in court.

I argued that Michael owed me money for at least spousal maintenance because he was working. Judge Everall remembered my appeal. He had seen documents of Michael taking over the property and issued new shares for the company under his and his mother's name. I emphasized that if Michael had not sold the property, it was due to his own doings and the ongoing criminal investigation against him, which had complicated the matter in Guatemala. I had evidence to indicate that Michael was renting the property with the aid of his friends from Century21. He was benefiting from thousands of US Dollars collecting in rent. Michael was putting my well-being, and economic situation, in a dangerous position and no one seemed to acknowledge that.

I also filed a court application requesting the court reinforcement to the disclosure of Michael's US taxes and Foreign Bank Account Reporting (FBAR) disclosures in conjunction with the above. But Judge Everall did not seem or care to understand my second application. I got

CHAPTER 12: DISCRIMINATION

told that I could not accuse Michael of owing me money by seeking help from the court to back up my claims with tax documents. I knew Michael was working. I emphasized not seeking Michael's US taxes to prove he was working. I asked the judge to look for evidence in my bundle, but he refused, and my evidence remained on his desk untouched.

I argued that Michael did not get dismissed from work in December 2018. "Mr. Hieb got discharged from his job in January, your Honor."

To what triggered a smile from the judge as if what I was saying was a joke.

"Oh, Mrs. Hieb, the things you say."

Judge Everall stated that Michael didn't owe me any money. My application to obtain Michael's US tax returns was dismissed and actually never dealt with, so it got shoved into limbo.

My arguments dismissed without merit. The court imposed a cost order to pay for the other party's legal fees. The disdainful glance I received from Joshua Viney was chilling. He requested the judge for a speedy reaction to their non-molestation order application against me. Michael's legal team consulted each other for a short moment, then the Barrister urged the judge to help them expedite the application.

The judge replied that they had to hurry to take care of the other details because he would not be in court much longer, meaning he intended to retire soon. I froze and felt like crying as there was not much else for me to do. I pressed my pen so hard that it broke in two and cut my hand.

When I thought things would finally start turning towards the light, the familiar feeling of emptiness invaded me again. I felt sad and could not stop thinking that if we are angel spirits in heaven, and it is our choice to come into this world, I must have been a foolish one to raise my hand to take on the ride.

Even getting the transcript for this court hearing was a massive obstacle. I had chosen another company to transcribe the hearing, which I was paying for, and the choice was mine. But after three weeks the company I picked complained about not receiving the court's tape for the hearing.

Finally, after many follow-up attempts, I was instructed to deal with Opus2 International Ltd. I knew this was the firm which usually worked with Payne Hicks Beach and I wanted to avoid them at all costs. Unfortunately the Central Family Court gave me no option but to deal with them.

It is sad to see how citizens like you and me receive such a high bar to meet the mark. When do we have a say? When can we get our voices heard and changes made? Our society is impregnated with corrupt people in power. Where is the desire to grow and get better? Only together we can make significant changes and overcome ineptitude. Why so much greed? How long will it take for us to wake up and say no more?

CHAPTER 12: DISCRIMINATION

The Regulators

As I mentioned before, an investigation was triggered with the Solicitors Regulation Authority for my concerns to be investigated. There was one document that the investigator found to be of interest. That document was the Century21 Sale Contract. Karma exists and has a way of working things out. The mentioned document, which at one point created so many problems and was used as an instrument to derail my legal matter, was coming back, this time to assist justice.

The SRA investigator began requesting information. He received all the necessary details and narratives from me to back up my points. And so, the investigative process began. A set of interviewing questions prepared and sent to the other party. To absolve themselves from the inquiry, Michael's solicitors most likely asked him to send a letter to the SRA investigator. In it, he stated that he had indeed issued and signed the Century21 sale contract and that District Judge Mulkis, already knew about it since the final court hearing of December 2018. When I called to follow up on the matter, the investigator told me about the letter Michael had sent. Convinced that the issue was already settled and done, he proceeded to finish the investigation. Remember the forensic expert I mentioned before? As far as reality goes, District Judge Mulkis stated during the final court appointment that even after the forensic evidence, he remained convinced I had signed the Century21 sale contract.

The investigator then communicated that he would dismiss and close my complaint. He repeated what Michael wrote in the letter, and believed that Judge Mulkis had already settled the issue during the final court hearing. I replied with objections and provided evidence, indicating that the Century21 sale contract was listed in the disputed items for the appeal in July 2019.

I could not get the SRA investigator to listen. It seems as if evidence meant nothing to him. After I was brushed off, I requested a copy of the letter sent by Michael. Mr. Holden, the investigator, replied that he could not release a copy without the consent of Michael's lawyers. I argued that if Michael confirmed the matter was settled in court in 2018, it made the letter part of my case file. So, I asked him to request permission to share it. A week went on, and the solicitors did not reply to the SRA investigator. I had to get in touch with Michael's solicitors at Payne Hicks Beach for an unrelated matter. In my email included a requested the favor for them to reply to the investigator who was waiting for their feedback.

Michael is not a solicitor, neither was he investigated; why did his solicitors ask him to send the letter directly to the investigator? Why did the investigator allow the interaction with Michael? Why not ask for the solicitors to send him Michael's letter? I can only assume that the reason was to play the blame game. If Ben Perry-Smith and Joshua Moger had delivered Michael's evidence to the investigator and later proven fraudulent, they would have to face accountability. But if Michael sent it directly to the investigator and his statement passed as reliable, he would have helped absolve his solicitors from the investigation. In exchange, if caught submitting false information, he would have walked away, causing little to no damage as his solicitors could have claimed not knowing what was in the letter.

After calling Payne Hicks Beach regarding my email and my request for them to get back to the SRA investigator, I called Mr. Stuart Holden. He seemed nervous and spoke in a cracking, fast-paced voice. He confirmed receiving a message from Payne Hicks Beach solicitors. Mr. Holden stated that my case was closed. He could no longer speak with me about the matter and not contact him anymore. Mr. Holden left me feeling very disconcerted. I was left thinking he had been intimidated.

These are solicitors who work for "strong" legal firms and are non-deserving of being called high-pedigree firms, rather ultra-expensive and extremely well-connected. Some have strange things going on in their firms, for instance, a solicitor and partner from Payne Hicks Beach who apparently appeared on the wanted list of the FBI. Nevertheless, the praises in James' awards and accolades on his work profile read as follows:

> James was listed in the Citywealth Leaders Honors List 2019,[29] for contentious trusts, cultural property and landed estates, "…genial, charming yet uncompromisingly efficient…If trusts and estates were a martial art, then partner James Bacon would be a black belt."[30]

I can only wonder how many more people benefited from the legal-illegal doings diverting the course of law. One of the articles mentioned a solicitor complaining about the Solicitors Regulation Authority for not doing enough to protect solicitors. When I read the article, I had to stop and think twice; why would solicitors need protection from the mere entity regulating them?[31]

Important Things in Life

I learned that even the best swimmers can get trapped in dangerous whirlpools. Realizing that if I was already getting pulled by the centripetal force, I must get to the bottom and catapult myself back up again. Vortexes in the shape of emergencies were coming from all over. My unconditional love for my children steered my focus to help them first, so I was there when my son Steven needed me. My eldest son was severely ill. His gentle soul had suffered from Michael's abuse just like his other siblings. Steven struggled to handle the situation at home and began bottling up his pain, which resulted in him refusing to speak about his trauma. After leaving for university, he and his younger brother decided to stay away from home unless Michael was not around. Steven began suffering from depression, leaving him unable to trust his partners, ending in broken relationships.

In February 2021, I almost lost Steven. With my meagre resources, I flew to New York and remained with my son for about a month. I believe love can help heal, so I

CHAPTER 12: DISCRIMINATION

gave my son all I had. My heart ached to see him facing such a struggle. It hurts me terribly when I think back on what he experienced. So many times, I prayed that I would wake up from the nightmare and go back to when we were happy, and he was my happy green leprechaun. When Steven was about seven years old, all shades of green outfits filled his closet. He loved green so much that I wondered if he was color blind.

Steven has a contagious lovely smile. He spent hours cooing to a Chinese painting on rice paper when he was a baby. Then, when he was about six months old, he would fix his sight on the same artwork and keep a whole conversation with unbreakable attention. I always thought he spoke to angels, and they replied.

When I returned to London, Steven was stable and in good spirits. I knew that very soon we would see each other again. He had his good friend, younger brother, sister and my brother near him; it was a matter of following his progress and keeping an eye on his mental well-being with the help of a great team of experts. I have nothing but praise for New York-Presbyterian/Weill Cornell Hospital for the care they continue to provide to my son. I must also mention my gratitude towards the health system in place since the Obama Administration and now under President Biden. Thank you to Governor Cuomo for his leadership during the pandemic and the love you hold for New York. I never doubted your integrity. It is often said that good news makes no news as your acquittal of the accusations you faced was never well publicized. Was it to get you off politics because you were too good?

As soon as I returned to London, my legal crusade continued. I became fed up with the family court and legal system. My thoughts were with the women I met in similar situations to mine. I learned about a woman whose young child was getting used to making her abandon a financial settlement fight. Her husband, a financier, was abusive and overly controlling. He wanted the custody of their four-year-old girl. This man also had economic power and high-end solicitors, similar to my case. Did the court allow this Iranian mother to keep her child? She said to be facing two choices, getting spousal maintenance or keeping her daughter. It was scary to learn the struggles that many women faced in the family court and how regular cruelty takes place when deciding the faith of the economically challenged.

While listening to a song by Kevin Morby called *I Was on Time*, I began to cry and remembered my mother. A champion woman, mother of five. Mom had gone through two civil wars, one earthquake and became a widow in her early twenties. Yet, she was a shining light and leader in her community; her door was always open to those in need. I learned from mom to give and not expect, to love and care. I wanted her to see me coming out alive from the whirlpool; I wanted her to feel proud of me. The song's lyrics inspire me to pick up myself again and keep fighting to get to the finishing line. Thanks Mom, you are always with me.

I don't think anyone can say that I did not seek help, alternative options or didn't try. I knocked on so many doors but they all got slammed in my face. Life has a way of working things up. In a way, the very same people who abused, ignored and turned me into a victim are why I began writing my memoirs. Hopefully, with your help, my voice will amplify, reaching far and wide to benefit many, not just me. So, I would say to the broken, exhausted, and in despair—raise your head, pick up the pieces and determine to be victims no more.

The Legal of the Illegal

With evidence of the fraudulent statement provided by Michael to the SRA's investigator, I opted to again contact the Metropolitan Police. After their entangle protocol, I finally got in contact with a Detective Constable. For the first time in a while, I had someone efficient, knowledgeable and willing to acknowledge to my complaints. I went through the long list of items that led to the different issues with the solicitors and investigation conducted by the Solicitors Regulation Authority.

After several days of performing a comprehensive evaluation, Detective Constable Parker accepted to work on my case. I proceeded to apply in the Central Family Court for the disclosure of the letter sent by Michael to the investigator to help absolve his solicitors from the SRA's inquiry. When Michael's solicitors learned about my application, they threatened me with a general civil restraint order (GCRO).

The judge assigned to the case happened to be HH Judge Gibbons; the very same judge who in 2018 allowed the "Pound per Pound" court order to help pay for my solicitors and the one who had allowed Michael to rely on the Century21 sale contract to get his independent property valuation in Guatemala.

However, instead of the designated Judge Gibbons, I ended up with another judge. A highly criticized and controversial judge in the Family Court. A year before, Judge Tolson dismissed a claim of rape after stating that the woman did not close her legs tight enough. And now, the same judge was overseeing my case. During the process, my correspondence to the court and emails to the court's desk for appointments began to go missing. My desperate attempt to contact Judge Gibbons' clerks was fruitless. I had to complain to the Central Family Court about what had happened.[32]

During the court appointment, I was scared and relieved at the same time. I felt that I had reached the summit of Sisyphus' hill and had Detective Constable D. Parker willing to contact the Judge and, if necessary, take the matter for a separate investigation under his jurisdiction. I thought having valuable information and reason to sound alarm bells for a significant investigation about how Michael's solicitors maliciously interfered in my legal matter.

As indicated, DC Parker called Judge Tolson to introduce himself before the court appointment. During the hearing on 20 June 2020, I already had solid evidence that Michael was working. He had left his financial consulting company Bahlam Core Ltd dormant, and launched another Fintech named Equities in Hong Kong SAR with a new partner, Mr. Benj Roberts, acting as Chief Technology Officer. Listed as Director and CEO (Chief Executive Officer) was Michael Hieb. I guess he learned how to move money through the system by making underwriting loans with his platform in South Asia. Michael had or was still working with AMPLIFI Credit Technology in Hong Kong, as Director of IT as well as being an investor.

Michael was advertising his position as Director of Data Systems all over the internet besides being an investor at AMP Credit Technology before the company changed its name to AMPLIFI. He had been working with AMP and then AMPLIFI since early 2019! AMP Credit Technology was also proud to display its European FinTech Award. Such evidence helped cement that successful companies don't lose 90% of their value in one year as Michael have claimed.

The hurdle of carrying and preparing court bundles and their distribution to the respective parties continued. I was self-representing the court-appointed Payne Hicks Beach to handle the details of our video conference. From the beginning, there was misinformation about video calls. Michael's solicitors kept asking for my phone number, which for obvious safety reasons, I kept private. I insisted on directly dealing with the court's clerk instead. But Payne Hicks Beach continued to feed me the information. As told, the call would be via Skype. Not until the very last minute did I find out the call would be via Skype for Business, which I didn't have due to monetary resources. The meeting was starting, and I could not get through. I was frantically trying to contact the court's clerk, who finally replied to my messages and kindly connected me via voice only.

When I finally managed to join the court hearing, Judge Tolson was irritated with me for being disrespectful and joining the hearing late. But His Honor did not seem to care when I tried to explain my mundane problems. Michael and his team had all the necessary equipment and technology, yet Michael hid behind a black screen. My sixth sense told me that he was not alone. The law requires only the persons involved to be in the room, wherever the room is. Was his mistress in the room with him? Did she want to hear me cry and struggle in court? Monsters feed on negativity and pain. Did you enjoy it, Lina?

When the judge asked why Michael was not on the screen, his barrister Joshua Viney replied,

"Mr. Hieb is present, your Honor. As you can see, his name is at the bottom of the screen."

The judge seemed fine with that; who was I to say otherwise. Judge Tolson began with his questions. The other party went first and started their usual criticism of me. As required, I had statements written summarizing the purpose and points to pursue disclosure of documents and application for spousal maintenance, and a chronology to help the judge during the court appointment.

By then, I had learned about a particular program that helps prepare court bundles. I had two, which cost me about £300 to print plus the price of the binders. I also had to have one on me, to help the judge navigate through different tabs and pages.

CHAPTER 12: DISCRIMINATION

When my turn came, the judge didn't want to see my evidence bundle. The other party had argued that I had too many applications dismissed without merit. Of course, such a statement is untrue, but then again, at that point, I knew that Michael's legal team has the bad habit of forgetting accuracy when it is not convenient to them. As a result, I wasted countless court hours and valuable resources, costing significant amounts to citizens.

The other party's court bundle includes a long list of my court applications. Mr. Joshua Viney recited some of the items. I heard how he told the judge that my non-molestation order got dismissed without merit when in reality was an extempore as well as my application with Mr. Justice Williams, which I had withdrawn. Viney claimed I was only attempting to continue my campaign to ruin Michael's reputation. Once again, the barrister tried to demonstrate my ill character. And, of course, his usual lies did not surprise me.

When I learned that Michael's lawyers launched an application to stop me from filing further proceedings in court, I panicked. I filed a mirror application a few days before the court hearing to prevent them from doing so. Judge Tolson laughed when it was brought up in court by the other party. The judge told me that I was leaning on the wrong tree. Barrister Joshua Viney jumped to say it was my vindictive character. The judge replied that I was playing a tit-for-tat game. My ignorance of the law was evident. I had made a mistake; nonetheless, the judge deemed that application dismissed without merit, adding it to the pile presented to him.

Judge Tolson asked what I had against the solicitors from Payne Hicks Beach.

"What have the solicitors done to you, Mrs. Hieb?"

I replied, "That they haven't done anything directly to me, but it was rather what they had done to my legal matter. They have acted illicitly and purposely derailed my case and misled the court. Even further, your Honor, now that they are getting investigated by the Solicitors Regulation Authority, after providing false evidence. Ben Parry-Smith and Joshua Moger had their client, Mr. Hieb, send a letter of falsehoods to help them get absolved from the SRA investigation ..."

"Mrs. Hieb", said Judge Tolson, "If I were to grant you a disclosure of the document you seek, what would you do with that information?",

"I would go to Crown Court, your Honor, and declare fraud. Since the beginning of my litigation, Mr. Hieb has committed fraud, and no one seemed to want to pay attention to that."

As soon as Joshua Viney could speak, he told the judge, "Imagine, your Honor, the massive expense my client would have to face to defend himself. Your Honor, my client's reputation would get destroyed, and he will lose all opportunities to source a job after such a claim!"
Joshua Viney then began with the name-calling.

"Mrs. Hieb is a vindictive woman. She just wants to harm her ex-husband because she's jealous. Our client is in a happy relationship with a new partner."

Without knowing much about me or having any understanding that I was the one who applied for divorce in the first place, the judge appeared not to listen to my arguments, and neither did he inspect evidence from two court bundles, but instead agreed with Joshua Viney.

When recording the judgement, it got stated that, understandably, litigants-in-person should not say certain things in court. But as is the case sometimes, doing so could harm their case. I had made a mistake by being honest and was getting punished for doing so.

During the judgement, the judge called me creative and the maker of a vicious campaign; and told me I was abusing court resources and putting my ex-husband under stress. I felt terrorized by Judge Tolson—he spoke in a highly condescending voice and told me to stop talking four times in a row. Even though I mentioned the statements from my ex-husband's barrister were false, Judge Tolson accepted them. He dismissed my reference to a matter already proven untrue in past court hearings. He opted to record that my behavior was destructive but did not care to seek proof of what the barrister had accused me. It was obvious that he didn't want to listen to my arguments, but provided plenty of opportunities for the other side to present theirs. He also asked only specific questions to me, which didn't allow me to provide evidence and fully express my points. I felt that my ignorance of legal procedures was taken advantage of.

The Court denied the importance of the investigation to clarify essential items that derailed my divorce matter and blocked it, by granting my ex-husband a civil restraint order. I got labelled with dangerous behavior. Judge

Tolson dismissed my applications without merit. Unless he was willing to permit me to file future applications, I was forbidden to do so. The Judge confirmed that I could not continue with the police investigation, and that He will call Detective Constable Parker to let him know. He degraded, embarrassed, and intimidated me with his comments and accusations concerning the case. He mocked me for putting the name of Michael's two solicitors in the application for disclosure when they were not even part of my proceedings. He ignored crucial facts previously overlooked by other judges and Judge Everall.

That was a lot to take, and I felt small and desperate. I was losing my last chance. Then, the verdict began, and my tears started to pour. I could guess what the Judge would say. And the Judge began,

"NO, Mrs. Hieb, I will not grant you the release of the document you seek. After all, these two solicitors are not even part of your divorce matter, which is over, and you lost. There have been three high judges who previously rejected your other applications."

I felt that Judge Tolson ignored the point that my application was not related to my divorce issue but rather about fraud and disclosure, hence including Michael as the first respondent and the two solicitors as second respondents. The document Michael gave to the SRA investigator was the evidence to prove the falsehood of the Century21 Sale Contract.

I was biting my tongue and wanted to scream. When I got a moment, and the judge addressed me, I remarked that he didn't understand; I aimed to expose crime, not be

CHAPTER 12: DISCRIMINATION

vindictive. It had to get done to make things right. But he didn't appear to care.

It was weeks before I could think clearly and manage my anxiety attacks. On my mind were my three children. I had a recurring dream of Steven smiling and asking me to follow him. I would wake up in a panic, thinking something was wrong with him. I called or sent a message just to hear,

"Mom, I was thinking about you just now."

My problems were minor compared to those of others, so I would wake up the next day grateful for who I am and what I had and kept going.

On 27 September 2020, I proceeded to request permission to appeal HHJ Tolson's judgment at the High Court of Justice Family Division. Due to the pandemic, all interactions were made on paper and online. An explanation was required as to why my application references and valid points were not made immediately and on time. My submission ended up not being sufficient and explicit. My application was dismissed totally without merit by The Honorable Mr. Justice Cohen based on not having found technical grounds. Unfortunately, I am not a barrister or a solicitor to know how to point out injustice correctly.

I knew that if solicitors got reviewed, so too must judges. So, I looked until I found where and how. I began my complaints against District Judge Mulkis, Judge Everall and Judge Tolson. I gathered all evidence, narrated events, provided documentation and waited. My objections were controversial and proved the need for significant changes that need to take place in the Central Family Court. I believe the vast discretionary power held by judges should be earned by merit and peer review, not automatically granted. There is discrimination in court towards women, self-representing parties, and foreigners. There is also abuse of influence and connections by dishonest legal firms and their crew, who seem so comfortable thinking no one will ever find out about their wrongdoings because, until present, that's been the case.

The Judiciary Conduct Investigations Office dismissed all my complaints. In July 2020, I appealed their decision to the Judicial Appointments and Conduct Ombudsman, Paul Kernaghan CBE QPM, who also rejected my appeals. Two of the judges stepped down from their roles around this time. Judge Tolson QC left his role on 21 August 2020. Judge Mark Everall QC retired as a circuit judge on 3 June 2020. District Judge Mulkis, a highly appealed judge, continues to serve in the Central Family Court in London.[33]

Thanks to the miscarriage of justice, Michael has been vicious with his illicit behavior, leaving me with a dangerous and uncertain future. So, for now, and as far as I can, I will continue my battle attempting to survive the criminal accusations made by Michael and his illicit lawyer Oscar Estuardo Paiz Lemus, and the injustice from the Central Family Court.

The 'Secret' Family Court: Fact or Fiction[34] by His Honor Clifford Bellamy is a must-read book. This book could not have been timelier. It came just as the then current President of the Family Division Sir James Munby, launched a wide ranging Transparency Review, and family law practitioners and organizations have been addressing their minds to the very same subject matter in forming their responses to his call for evidence.

But the questions it grapples with are not new. The book's title refers to a decades-old accusation from the media and others, such as campaign groups, that the family courts operate a system of "secret justice", administered "behind closed doors", in which draconian orders affecting parents and children are shielded from public scrutiny—and, by implication, accountability.

Chapter 13

Reflections

The year 2020 made me reflect on the importance of love, family, our lives, health and the simple things in life. My birthday is 21 March; England went into lockdown on 20 March. As soon as I heard about National Health Service (NHS) first responders' program, I signed up. I took the initiative to provide aid to older people. There were many tasks, such as picking up medicine, delivering food, making checkup calls, or talking. When I went to the court hearing with Judge Tolson in June 2020, I had accumulated over 43 hours of helping the NHS. Preparing documents for the court was difficult; almost everything was closed.

I couldn't get to my children, especially my son Steven. I remember waking up on my birthday on a beautiful sunny day. The light invaded my bedroom and wrapped my legs with its warm rays. I love sunny days. Cherry trees and flowers were blossoming alike and birds happily chirped outside. I had very little in my fridge and no bread, but I had coffee which made my day. I toasted to life, health and success. Even though I was not close to winning my case, I was winning in life. I had become a better person, regained self-love, learned to smile again and calm my mind. By taking a practical approach to the pandemic, I thought that if all went to hell and death was imminent; I wanted to go while helping others. So, I began roaming the streets by collecting groceries and prescriptions and jogging simultaneously. I managed to remain healthy, got my three vaccinations, had no adverse side effects or pain whatsoever and, as far as I know, didn't get COVID.

London was experiencing a beautiful spring and summer in 2020. Four beautiful months of gorgeous sunny and warm weather. I stopped feeling alone and remember getting the best sleep I'd had in a long time. For once, I didn't have to keep up my guard to defend myself from others; we were all in the same situation. Creation and nature hold great hidden powers waiting for us to unveil. Our mind is more significant than the material body, and our spirit is infinite. I became a good listener, and I began to meditate, leading me to the incredible truth of who am I and why am I here. I also discovered the sound of silence—and it is beautiful!

It was harrowing going through the second scare of almost losing Steven in November 2021. During that period, Steven and I spent two months together, him recovering and I giving more love and anything else I could. Up to date, I can report that he continues with experimental medicine and is soon to go on the waiting list for an organ

CHAPTER 13: REFLECTIONS

transplant. If a partial transplant is possible and our blood type and other medical details deem us compatible, I will be able to help my son further. We have witnessed Steven embracing life again and that alone is a miracle. His two siblings, my younger brother, a handful of his friends, and I are ready to support him, and we are all looking forward to seeing Steven healthy and smiling again. He is keen on sharing his experience to help others overcome serious health conditions and turn a horrid experience into a positive outcome. I pray for Steven to continue his progress and don't give up.

I long for Michael to stop using Mercedes to hurt me and extract information, so I can hold her in my arms again to catchup with her "baby time". She is currently studying in the USA, living in unacceptable accommodation. According to her brothers who have visited her, she is in an apartment infested with rats. She often borrows money for food and clothing from her brothers and sister-in-law. I was in disbelief when I learned that she usually does not get loans. I got told that the reason was to make Michael take responsibility for his child instead of dumping her after he used her against me. My heart aches when I think of my daughter going through so much, and at the right time, I will fight for her to obtain a tuition and living expenses court ordered by the Central Family Court. During divorce litigation I asked Mercedes to insist for one, but she said that her father will not fail her, but he did. Michael has falsely convinced her that he has no money. Mercedes will wake up soon and stop trusting her abuser's lies. I will be there to hold my child's hand so we can begin healing together.

David, my younger son, changed his last name as he could not bear passing the Hieb last name to his soon-to-be-born child.

Michael is currently working as Chief Risk Officer for Segantii Capital Management Limited in Hong Kong since November 2020. He is also listed on the NYU University of Shanghai to the MS in Data Analytics & Business Computing Advisory Board. What a fraud.

In Guatemala, Michael has gone as far as tampering with the signature of District Judge Mulkis in a legal document, faking a name and seal of a court interpreter from Central Family Court. In some documents sent to Guatemala, Joshua Moger appears with a variation of his name instead of the one used in the Central Family Court of England. As the criminal court progressed and plaintiffs continued to justify their claims in court against Michael and Oscar Estuardo Paiz Lemus, the pair began to feel the investigation's impact. So to gain time, the evil duo filed a countersuit in May 2020, claiming they were the victims of slander. I am unsure if they are delusional or inept but who could explain or predict criminal minds? Their law suit is against the rightful shareholder and dragged me plus two corporate lawyers who had nothing to do with the ongoing proceedings against Michael and Paiz Lemus. Michael was wrong to think that the corporate lawyers would abandon their clients with their ridiculous lawsuit.

For me it was an unpleasant surprise, because I had to source a defense lawyer and travel to Guatemala to declare

CHAPTER 13: REFLECTIONS

in court. Unfortunately for Michael, my legal defense is doing a great job. The unanticipated expenses caused me to borrow again, leaving me further in debt. I often contemplate how I could have used the money to help Steven instead of wasting it in Michael's fruitless claims. He is aware of our son's condition, but he does not care. I can expect nothing good when dealing with such a heartless man.

Despite the horrific articles in the news regarding police brutality and power of abuse in the US and England, reports keep popping up with yet more of the same situations. I once believed that British law was solid and the fairest; I woke up and saw the reality of its inefficiency and ineptitude in preventing such atrocities. A 12-year-old rape victim took her own life directly after an interview with a police officer who had previously discouraged her from bringing forward a criminal complaint and subsequently failed to properly investigate it; her mother had told Sky News. Imagine how desperate you must be to take your own life. Andrew Clark, 38, and his younger brother Jason Clark, 35, were found guilty of a series of horrific sexual assaults on children last year after committing sexual assaults over a 25-year period.[35]

We live in dangerous times and in a society of double standards. People in command and some in charge of our safety cannot be trusted.[36] Moreover, in February 2022, the head of police resigned when confronted with all the accusations of the misbehavior of her staff; she quit. But quitting her job did not fix the misogyny left behind. No wonder she's smiling. In line for a £575,000 payout and a

£160,000-a-year taxpayer-funded pension pot, Cressida Dick is set to put her feet up at her £1m country home and enjoy a leisurely life like her predecessor Bernard Hogan-Howe. It is nothing else but a disgrace! What about the victim attacked, the victims killed and their families waiting for accountability?[37]

Politicians quit; others don't even do that and continue to eat from our taxes until is evident they have to pack and go. And some don't even get questioned until there is a leak exposing their wrongdoing, mismanagement, abuse of power, and waste of valuable resources. So, it's crucial to understand that it is not a resignation from work that victims expect. We, victims in general, want and need accountability. The word corruption has gotten to the roots of almost all organizations public and private, and it seems to be the new norm. This is wrong! Constantly we are forced into doing things we disagree with, and it is time for us to wake up, slowly but surely.

It is spring of 2022; the sun again shines with splendor. The days are getting longer. Reflecting at some of the things I learned during the past four years are that stacked up court bundles create an excellent ergonomic angle to place my laptop. Most in the social sector helping victims and the needy stretch themselves beyond the call of duty to help their clients. Many of these people don't get paid fairly or get treated with the respect they deserve. Many criminals snatch mobile phones in front of police stations. At the same time, yet another set of female students lined

CHAPTER 13: REFLECTIONS

up at Islington Police Station to place their complaint about stolen phones. Would they get told as they told me, that I made too many complaints? That drug dealers and buyers go to playgrounds, sports and recreational grounds to sell, as police are usually absent from these places. I achieve living on £10 a week eating healthy, fresh veggies and fruit. I also learned not to lose my mind while living in assisted housing infested with antisocial social behavior and lack of accountability from the perpetrators and the housing association. Grounding is a fascinating healing tool hidden from our view. Jogging and walking are great to keep my heart, soul and mind in good shape and happy. I also learned that newspapers don't care about your story unless it is already a tragedy. Criminals eventually get caught, and bad people never win.

With love.

Prevail is now my name.

Notes

(1) Jalāl al-Dīn Muḥammad Rūmī (Rumi), *Power of Positivity*. Published online: March 22, 2020. https://www.powerofpositivity.com/rumi-quotes-transform-your-life/

(2) Nature 553, 252 (2018) 09 January 2018. DOI: https://doi.org/10.1038/d41586-018-00413-x

(3) Stephen Schlesinger and Stephen Kinzer. "Bitter Fruit: The Story of the American Coup in Guatemala". Harvard University Press; 2nd edition (23 Dec. 2005). ISBN: 978-0674019300

(4) Eduardo Galeano. "Open Veins of Latin America: Five Centuries of the Pillage of a Continent". Serpent's Tail; Main edition (21 May 2009). ISBN: 978-1846687426

(5) José Julián Martí Pérez (January 28, 1853 – May 19, 1895) was an important figure who is considered a Cuban national hero because of his role in the liberation of his country from Spain and Latin American literature. He was very politically active and is considered an important philosopher and political theorist. Through his political activity and writings, he became a symbol of Cuba's bid for independence from the Spanish Empire in the 19th century, and is referred to as the "Apostle of Cuban Independence". From a young age, he dedicated his life to the promotion of liberty, political independence for Cuba, and intellectual independence for all Spanish Americans. His death was used as a cry for Cuban independence from Spain by both the Cuban revolutionaries and other Cubans who were previously reluctant to start a revolt.

(6) Davies, Janey. "The Human Heart Has a Mind of Its Own, Scientists Find." Learning Mind, September 16, 2016. https://www.learning-mind.com/the-human-heart-mind/.

(7) Sanders, Laura. "A New 3-D Map Illuminates the 'Little Brain' within the Heart: Nerve Cells in the Organ Are Poorly nderstood." Science News, June 2, 2020. https://www.sciencenews.org/article/new-3-d-map-illuminates-little-brain-nerve-cells-within-heart.

(8) Davies, Janey. "The Human Heart Has a Mind of Its Own, Scientists Find." Learning Mind, September 16, 2016. https://www.learning-mind.com/the-human-heart-mind/.

(9) Tupac Amaru Shakur; born Lesane Parish Crooks, June 16, 1971 – September 13, 1996), also known as Tupac, 2Pac, and/or Makaveli, was an American rapper. He is widely considered to be one of the most influential rappers of all time. Tupac is among the best-selling music artists, having sold over 75 million records worldwide. Much of his music has been noted for addressing contemporary social issues that plagued inner cities, and he is considered a symbol of activism against inequality.

(10) "Hope Water International (HWI) was launched in 2017 from Hope Water Project (HWP) as an effort to have a wider reach and impact on individuals, churches, and organizations to help provide access to clean water worldwide." https://www.hopewaterinternational.org/

(11) Shanon Thomas is a US-based Certified Clinical Trauma Professional (CCTP). Her primary area of specialty is recovery from abuse in all its forms. She has an international bestselling book, *Healing from Hidden Abuse: A Journey Through the Stages of Recovery from Psychological Abuse*, ranked #1 Self-Help (Abuse) and #1 Hot New Release Self-Help (Abuse) on Amazon.com. URL: https://southlakecounseling.org/

(12) Thomas, Shannon. "Shannon Thomas Quotes." Pinterest, September 11, 2022. https://www.pinterest.co.uk/hiddenabuse/shannon-thomas-quotes/.

(13) Connelly, Thomas. "Frustrated Family Judge Who Banged Hand on Desk Was 'Sarcastic and Condescending'." Legal Cheek, March 21, 2019. https://www.legalcheek.com/2019/03/frustrated-family-judge-who-banged-hand-on-desk-was-sarcastic-and-condescending/.
(14) HM Courts & Tribunals Service, Ministry of Justice, and Dominic Raab MP. "'Blame Game' Ends as No-Fault Divorce Comes into Force." GOV.UK., April 6, 2022. https://www.gov.uk/government/news/blame-game-ends-as-no-fault-divorce-comes-into-force.
Another useful article: "No-Fault Divorce - a Complete Guide - Find the UK's Best Divorce Solicitors." Wiselaw, September 14, 2022. https://www.wiselaw.co.uk/divorce/no-fault-divorce-complete-guide/.
(15) "England and Wales: Outgoing Judge Sir James Munby Describes as 'Woefully Indaequate' Help for Litigants in Person." Irish Legal News, July 30, 2018. https://www.irishlegal.com/articles/england-and-wales-outgoing-judge-sir-james-munby-describes-as-woefully-indaequate-help-for-litigants-in-person.
(16) Hellen, Nicholas. "Divorce 'Fighting Fund' for Spouses of Rich." The Sunday Times, September 29, 2018. https://www.thetimes.co.uk/article/divorce-fighting-fund-for-spouses-of-rich-0kcgp30xt.
(17) "Access to Justice Fund." Vardags, September 30, 2018. https://vardags.com/posts/britains-top-divorce-lawyer-launches-10-million-access-to-justice-loan-fund.
(18) Vardag, Ayesha. "The 'Super-Wealthy' Wives Trapped in a Gilded Cage." The Sydney Morning Herald, November 7, 2018. https://www.smh.com.au/business/the-economy/the-super-wealthy-wives-trapped-in-a-gilded-cage-20181107-p50eg3.html.
(19) Morgan-Bentley, Paul, and Alastair Good. "Action Fraud Investigation: Victims Misled and Mocked as Police Fail to

Investigate." News | The Times. The Times, August 16, 2019. https://www.thetimes.co.uk/article/action-fraud-investigation-victims-misled-and-mocked-as-police-fail-to-investigate-wlh8c6rs6.

(20) Bolch, John. "Sir James Munby Laments the State of the Family Court." Stowe Family Law, July 11, 2019. https://www.stowefamilylaw.co.uk/blog/2019/07/11/sir-james-munby-laments-the-state-of-the-family-court/.

(21) Martin, Alexander. "Semina Halliwell: Rape Victim, 12, Took Her Own Life Directly after Police Interview, Her Mother Tells Sky News." Sky News, April 6, 2022. https://news.sky.com/story/semina-halliwell-rape-victim-12-took-her-own-life-directly-after-police-interview-her-mother-tells-sky-news-12582931.

(22) Dawson, Joanna. "How Might Brexit Affect Human Rights in the UK? - House of Commons Library," December 27, 2019. https://commonslibrary.parliament.uk/how-might-brexit-affect-human-rights-in-the-uk/.

(23) MGI Midgley Snelling LLP. "Law Firms 'Not Doing Enough' to Prevent Money Laundering, says SRA." MGI Midgley Snelling LLP, September 10, 2019. https://www.midsnell.co.uk/law-firms-not-doing-enough-to-prevent-money-laundering-says-sra/.

(24) Rose, Neil. "Call to Protect Compliance Officers Who Report Solicitors to SRA." Legal Futures, October 7, 2018. https://www.legalfutures.co.uk/latest-news/call-to-protect-compliance-officers-who-report-solicitors-to-sra.

(25) Bray, Jonathon. "SRA Declares War on Toxic Cultures with New Guidance." Jonathon Bray. Industry Insights, February 10, 2022. https://www.jonathonbray.com/sra-declares-war-on-toxic-cultures-with-new-guidance/.

(26) Rimmer, Colin. "Solicitors Regulation Authority in £33m Cover-Up." Corruption UK, July 28, 2020. https://corruptionuk.org/solicitors-regulation-authority-in-33m-cover-up/.

(27) The Bar Standard Handbook, Ed. 4.6; 31 December 2020. https://www.barstandardsboard.org.uk/the-bsb-handbook.html

(28) Bolch, John. "Sir James Munby Laments the State of the Family Court." Stowe Family Law, July 11, 2019. https://www.stowefamilylaw.co.uk/blog/2019/07/11/sir-james-munby-laments-the-state-of-the-family-court/.

(29) "Payne Hicks Beach Lawyers Listed in Citywealth Leaders List 2019." Payne Hicks Beach, July 11, 2019. https://www.phb.co.uk/news/citywealth-leaders-list-2019.

(30) "James Bacon." Payne Hicks Beach, n.d. Quoted in Legal 500 UK 2022. https://www.phb.co.uk/our-people/profile/james-bacon.

(31) "Payne Hicks Beach Solicitors Partner James Bacon + Dechert Law Firm Insolvency Partner Paul J. Fleming + Pinsent Masons Insolvency Partner Nick Pike – FBI Los Angeles Assistant Director – DOJ 'Criminal Prosecution Files' – Dentons Chairman Joseph Andrew * DLA Piper Chairman Roger Meltzer * McDermott Will & Emery Partner Simon Goldring = Carroll Anglo-American Corporation Trust = Jones Day Managing Partner Stephen J. Brogan * Slaughter & May * Withersworldwide Chairman Ivan A. Sacks * Loeb & Loeb Chairman Kenneth R. Florin – FBI Los Angeles Biggest White Collar Organized Crime Bank Fraud Case in History." Rapid News Platform – Carroll Foundation Trust, n.d. https://news-carrolltrust.com/payne-hicks-beach-solicitors-fraud-offshore-tax-evasion-files-criminal-liability-carrolltrust-fbi-biggest-national-security-case/.

Further link: https://news-carrolltrust.com/wp-content/uploads/2014/10/A-08-211x300.jpg

(32) Fouzder, Monidipa. "High Court Condemns Leadership Judge's 'Obsolescent' View on Consent." Law Gazette, January 23, 2020. https://www.lawgazette.co.uk/news/high-court-condemns-leadership-judges-obsolescent-view-on-consent/5102818.article.

(33) Fouzder, Monidipa. "Family Judge Steps down from 'Thankless' Leadership Role." Law Gazette, August 11, 2020. https://www.lawgazette.co.uk/news/family-judge-steps-down-from-thankless-leadership-role/5105312.article.

(34) His Honor Clifford Bellamy, "The 'Secret' Family Court: Fact or Fiction". Bath Publishing; 1st edition (18 Mar. 2020). ISBN-13 : 978-1916431584

(35) Sherdley, Rebecca. "Vile Brothers Jailed for Horrific Sex Crimes Including Rape of a Child." mirror, April 6, 2022. https://www.mirror.co.uk/news/uk-news/vile-brothers-jailed-horrific-sex-26646109.

(36) Winter, Alex. "Met Police Cop Raped Two Women and Hit One with Bottle - but Won't Be Charged." The Sun, April 5, 2022. https://www.thesun.co.uk/news/18177398/met-police-raped-two-women-never-charged/.

(37) Fielding, James, and Andrew Young. "No Wonder She's Smiling! Cressida Dick in Line for a £575,000 Payout." Daily Mail Online. Associated Newspapers, February 11, 2022. https://www.dailymail.co.uk/news/article-10502543/No-wonder-shes-smiling-Cressida-Dick-line-575-000-payout.html.